UNDER HIS WINGS

UNDER HIS WINGS

Meeting the Spiritual Needs of the Mentally Disabled

ROBERT BITTNER

CROSSWAY BOOKS • WHEATON, ILLINOIS
A DIVISION OF GOOD NEWS PUBLISHERS

Under His Wings

Published by Crossway Books
a division of Good News Publishers
1300 Crescent Street
Wheaton, Illinois 60187

Cover photos: Special thanks to Shepherds of Union Grove, Wisconsin
for photos of Mary Sue Hayes, Tom Harrison,
Becky VanDuren, and Holly Ann and to Melmark Home
of Berwyn, Pennsylvania

First printing, 1994

Printed in the United States of America

Library of Congress Cataloging-in-Publication Data
Bittner, Robert. 1961-
    Under His wings: meeting the spiritual needs of th mentally
disabled / [Robert Bittner].
        p.   cm.
    Includes bibliographical references
1. Church work with the mentally handicapped. 2. Mentally
handicapped—Religious life. I. Title.
BV4460.2.B58 1994   261'.8'323—dc20   94-31611
ISBN 0-89107-805-3

02		01		00		99		98		97		96		95		94
15	14	13	12	11	10	9	8	7	6	5	4	3	2	1

For my sister
Barbara Jane Bittner
I write so that
I might understand

Table of Contents

Acknowledgments

A book of this nature cannot be written without the support and input of many, many people.

For their general encouragement, I want to thank the members of my writers' group back in Elgin, Illinois: Bernice Borzeka (who provided background information I would not otherwise have encountered), Sherrie Bryant, Janet Riehecky, Jack Tofari, and Judy Warner. And for her long-distance friendship and support, Rebecca Neason; you have been a blessing to me.

I especially am grateful to the more than seventy-five churches across the country that responded with honesty and insight to my survey and follow-up telephone calls regarding their current work with the mentally handicapped. Their experiences—both good and bad—are the backbone for the text; their willingness to share information made it possible.

My sincere appreciation goes to Charlene Heibert, representative of David C. Cook Publishing Company, for her kind permission in allowing me to include extensive material from David C. Cook Foundation publications.

A big thank you to my in-laws, Bill and Joyce Freeman of Charlotte, Michigan, for patiently allowing me to write in their attic during the two months while my wife and I were in house-moving limbo between Illinois and Michigan.

The lives and influence of my parents, Madison and Lois Bittner, have informed practically all of the personal content in this book. They have been examples of love, patience, and honest faith.

Lastly, I would not have been able to write this book without both the understanding and the patience of my wife, Sylvia. The former was a given when we married; the latter is growing.

Introduction

When coworkers and friends learned that I was writing a book, it was only natural for them to inquire about the topic. When I described it as being "about the spiritual needs of the mentally handicapped," many expressed pleasure, commenting that there probably was a real need for a book on that subject. But there was something else in their eyes, a look that hinted, "Okay, but why are *you* writing it?"

My interest in the spiritual needs of the mentally handicapped came to me naturally. I was raised in a Christian home (my father is a retired minister), and I have an older sister, Barbara, who is mentally disabled. Although I have over the years rebelled against both situations, I have no doubt that they both have had a profound impact on the growth of my Christian life. They have made me the person I am today.

As a result, I have come to believe that Christians have much to offer the mentally handicapped people who live among us—even as the handicapped have much to offer in return. Unfortunately, the opportunities for outreach and ministry are not all that obvious at first glance. Even Christians can miss seeing them. But I'm not willing to chalk that up to insensitivity or willful disregard. Instead, I think the reason is simply a lack of understanding regarding the needs and wants of this minority population. We avoid what we do not understand; and who without medical training, the thinking may go, can understand so varied a group of people? They are people with whom it is sometimes hard to communicate. People who probably don't share our backgrounds and experiences. People who sometimes, if we're honest about it, make us uncomfortable by their uniqueness.

The fact is, it is not all that difficult to recognize the spiritual needs of the mentally handicapped—and to take steps to meet them through ministry. It just requires the desire to look and *see*. Admitting that we do not reach out to them because we don't know what to say or how to teach them or how to answer the questions of others in our churches is the first positive step toward a vital ministry. The second step comes once we're willing to move beyond our apprehensions and fears to ask, Who are these people really, and what can I be doing to help them know God? That is what I mean by looking and *seeing*.

For instance, my sister, Barbara, is mildly disabled, with an IQ perhaps in the mid-sixties. (Seventy is considered the dividing line between a mental handicap and normality.) If you were to see her in a restaurant or at the movies, she would seem at first glance to be as normal as you or I. After all, she holds a forty-hour-a-week job, lives in her own apartment, walks to the local shopping center, and spends free time with friends and family. Look closer, though—take the time to know her as an individual—and the reality of her handicap comes into focus. Barbara works at a sheltered workshop for the handicapped, lives in a supervised apartment building, and has some difficulty with the simple math involved in making change. She is functional and relatively independent, conversationally shy but quick to laugh, and able to learn new information. And she represents the majority of mentally handicapped adults.

In the United States alone, there are five to seven million mentally handicapped men and women, boys and girls. For comparison, that is a mentally disabled population roughly equal in size to the population of New York City.

Some are severely handicapped and are under constant medical care. Others battle physical disabilities such as cerebral palsy and spina bifida, in addition to their mental handicaps. Some bear the physical characteristics of Down syndrome, while others can, like Barbara, pass through society without much notice.

Regardless of their condition, the mentally handicapped have spiritual needs, just as they have the more obvious physical and emotional needs. Christians can play an important role in helping to meet those needs by introducing the mentally disabled to the God of Scripture and by living lives that exemplify His accepting love for them in the real world. In the course of researching this book, I spoke with believers who did just that—who reached out to an often neglected group in the name of God. As a result, they formed relationships with people who challenged their assumptions, occasionally tested their patience, and enriched their faith. It is my conviction that you and your church can share in that experience.

The Christian church has come a long way from the days when Martin Luther could write of the mentally handicapped, "The Devil sits where their souls should have been." I think we have also moved beyond believing the opposite—that mentally disabled people are somehow specially "blessed" with the gift of pure innocence. Both ideas are equally dangerous. If we believe them to be devils, we will not respect them enough to speak to them of the Good News; we will avert our eyes and keep our distance. But if we believe them sanctified already, we will not fear for their souls. We will convince ourselves that even though they may be able to learn how to tie fishing lures, play a musical instrument, or perform in a church play, their disability somehow marks them holy and unaccountable in the eyes of God.

The fact is, the mentally handicapped are neither dev-ils nor angels. They are human beings, created in God's image and having many of our basic needs and desires, while also having special needs that are uniquely their own. To be perfectly frank, I did not always care about those needs. As an adolescent and young adult, I was embarrassed by or ashamed of my sister. Once I was old enough to understand Barbara's handicap, she ceased being simply my older sister and became my older, *retarded* sister—the sibling I tried to explain away when my friends visited, the "announcement" I felt obligated to make as soon as anyone asked whether I had any brothers or sisters.

I resented the many ways in which Barbara was not "normal." A "normal" sister, I believed, would have been able to help me over the hurdles of high school and first dates and the panic of leaving for college. I would have been able to share with her my concerns about making a living and finding a mate. I wanted counsel, encouragement, sup-port. Barbara could supply none of those, and I was angry about that. It didn't occur to me that scores of other "nor-mal" brothers and sisters never shared such idealized times together. I was frustrated by the fact that she wasn't the sis-ter I wanted her to be, the sister I thought she *should* be.

Looking back, I realize I was alone in my frustration. My parents had long since worked through any doubts or anger they had experienced following Barbara's birth, having set-tled comfortably into parental love and acceptance. Similarly, the people at church, who saw my family several times a week, were always encouraging my sister. They will-ingly talked *with* her rather than around her. They inte-grated her into their Sunday school classes. They welcomed her at Sunday morning worship. Ultimately, the example of their unconditional acceptance helped me mature into a love of my own.

That kind of loving Christian witness is still needed in our churches today. But it does not come easily without understanding the situation of the mentally disabled, what a mental handicap is, and what it does and does not mean. It does not come without a commitment to persevere. And it cannot come at all unless we make a prayerful effort to look beneath surface appearances and glimpse the real people we want to reach. My prayer is that this book, along with your eagerness and God's grace, will help you reach out to the mentally handicapped in love—leading them to the shelter and love discovered when we come under God's wings. The mentally handicapped will not be the only ones who win. I believe everyone who ministers to them will discover a deeper, more meaningful faith in the process.

Chapter 1

OPENING OUR HEARTS AND MINDS

For we were all baptized by one Spirit into one body—whether Jews or Greeks, slave or free—and we were all given the one Spirit to drink.

1 CORINTHIANS 12:13

What does it mean to be mentally handicapped? On the surface, the answer is easy. Whether the cause is disease, a birth defect, or brain damage, the result is a slowed down ability to learn. In a way it is as simple as that: to be mentally handicapped or disabled or retarded is to be a slow learner. Of course, this describes an incredible variety of people and personalities. One goal of this book is to move beyond surface definitions and to seek out the real-life faces, the flesh-and-blood people, behind what can become a generic label.

It seems that many of those normal people who take that first step find some special benefit from meeting the mentally handicapped. In fact, I would guess that we profit even in ways the mentally disabled do not. For instance, some people come away talking about how loving they can be; by working with the mentally handicapped, they've discovered a new facet to love. Others have described the

17

impact of the disabled's sense of humor, devotion, easygoing temperament, sincerity, or trust.

When I think about what it means to be mentally handicapped, one defining characteristic that comes to my mind is *courage*. The reason is a man named Terry Gazdik.

A PORTRAIT IN COURAGE

I don't remember when I first met Terry, but I do know that I have never forgotten him. He was short, about 5'4", with a barrel chest, a broad, round face, and long, thinning strands of black hair swept back with hair cream. His pug nose and thick arms made him look like a fighter. Maybe deep down he was—and maybe he had to be. People could lose patience talking to Terry. His slightly slurred speech required constant attention. And although he wore a hearing aid, he was always turning his good ear toward you, wrinkling his forehead, and barking, "What?" out of the side of his mouth. Even when he did hear you, there wasn't any guarantee your conversation would mean much to him. Technology helped his hearing, but it offered no assistance in coping with his mild retardation.

Thankfully, Terry didn't need much technology. He had his mother, a pugnacious woman herself, whose determination was instrumental in starting a sheltered-care workshop for the mentally handicapped in my hometown in southern Illinois. Through the training offered at that facility, many young adults—Terry included—were taught skills they could use outside the workshop, in the "real" world. That's why, when I remember Terry, I think of him first in terms of his courage. After several years, he graduated from the nurturing environment of the workshop and moved on to an unsheltered, unpredictable life as a part-time short-order cook. And he succeeded. Although he never moved away from home, he had his own bicycle, a regular paycheck, and his independence. Judging from his wide smiles and frequent chuckles, I think he thrived in the real world. Unfortunately, he did not get to stay in that world very long; Terry was still in his twenties when he died of a heart attack.

I was reminded of his real-world example not long ago when, while standing in line at a McDonald's restaurant, I noticed a girl with Down syndrome mopping up between the tables. Like Terry, she had courageously moved into the mainstream. I say "courageously" because this young woman concentrated on doing her job despite some customers' hushed asides and curious glances. Many of us who struggle against no obvious mental or physical handicaps know how deeply we can feel embarrassment when faced with others' insensitivity; it must take far more willpower to ignore those comments when you *know* you truly are different (a self-understanding that most mentally handicapped people have). I couldn't help seeking out her supervisor and thanking her for employing a mentally handicapped individual.

Our world is filled with many other mentally handicapped people who have much to share with all of us, whether an act of kindness, an example of love or courage, or a warm, ongoing relationship. Still, had it not been for having a mentally disabled sister—and for growing up in an environment where mental handicaps were nearly as normal as normality was—I have no doubt that my response to the mentally handicapped would have been different. I may have avoided eating at Terry's restaurant for fear that there might be something wrong with his cooking. I may have stared at the girl in McDonald's or felt she wasn't worth a second glance. Although I've been a committed Christian

for twenty years, I know how easy it is even now to stereo-
type, to judge, to turn away. I feel certain I'm not alone.

When I was working as a book editor with a Christian
publishing company, I had the privilege of editing a book
entitled *The Journey Through AIDS* by Debra Jarvis, an
ordained minister and AIDS counselor. The book was emotionally overwhelming for author and editor alike, being
filled with the stories of those who watched their relatives
and friends grapple with this terrible disease. But one section
of the book appeared to lapse into a kind of sweet senti-
mentality that just didn't seem to reflect the same weight as
the surrounding material, and I suggested to Debra that we
cut it out altogether. In it she had recommended that caregivers learn how to look at others with "soft eyes"; I
explained that the term "soft eyes" called to mind a certain
brand of impossibly doe-eyed ceramic figurines. Once she
stopped laughing, Debra turned serious, pointing out how
the concept of seeing with "soft eyes" had helped innumer-
able people she had counseled. It is an attitude that allowed
them to better see the worth and the need in every human
being, regardless of their physical or mental situation. In the
end I had to agree. The short passage remained in the book.

> Soft eyes are not the narrowed eyes of judgment or the
> bulging eyes of fear. They do not look out from
> beneath knitted brows of worry. Soft eyes are relaxed
> and open and clear. Soft eyes will allow you to see . . .
> right through to the heart of the person.

In retrospect, I see that her words echo Jesus' challenge
to love our neighbors as much as we love ourselves, to consider them just as useful, just as worthy to be in the world,
as we ourselves. I believe the same sentiment was behind the
Apostle Paul's statement in 1 Corinthians 12:13: "For we

were all baptized by one Spirit into one body—whether Jews or Greeks, slave or free—and we were all given the one Spirit to drink." Our commonality in Christ is of far greater importance than differences of race or social status *or mental aptitude*.

But to see that commonality, to open our eyes to the needs of the mentally handicapped, we have to remove the blinders that have restricted our understanding in the past.

STEPPING OUT OF THE DARK

Language, superstition, the creation of specialized institutions, and apathy and fear have all hindered our ability to discover the mentally handicapped on their own terms. Other "blinders" certainly exist; however, many will fall into these general categories. Identifying them will help us to move beyond them, trading false or naive assumptions for the facts about mental handicaps.

Language. Because my sister is ten years older than I am, I wasn't very involved in her life when she made her way through the public school system. Judging from my own experience, though, I doubt that she made it through unscathed by verbal assaults. What normal child hasn't faced the epithets "retard," "stupid," "ignoramus," and "idiot"? Children, we're told, can be cruel and insensitive. But what about their parents—or grandparents? It is not uncommon to find, even among books written within the last twenty years, labels like "mental defectives," "retardates," and "imbeciles." Today when we struggle with such politically correct labels as "developmentally disabled" and "mentally challenged," the bold language of the past sounds insensitive, uncaring.

Of course, words are just words, and all language

changes with time. But the words we use to describe the world around us directly affect our attitudes toward that world; that's as true in the nineties as it was in the twenties. While the phrase "mental defective" may have passed from common use, the attitude still remains, and it is still dangerous. It's a lot easier to write off someone who is "defective" than someone who is "handicapped." (On the other hand, labored descriptions like "developmentally disabled" and "mentally challenged" seem to me to be the verbal equivalent of keeping the mentally handicapped at bay, which is just as problematic.)

Through the continued insensitive use of language, we can blind ourselves to the rewards of knowing the mentally handicapped. We also handicap the mentally disabled even further, effectively denying them any chance to become valuable members of our society. As Gene Newman and Joni Eareckson Tada wrote in *All God's Children*, "People are not to be labeled 'retards' or 'cripples' or 'handicaps.' They are people who happen to have a physical or mental impairment that may or may not handicap them as they go about their daily routines."

I wholeheartedly agree. For the sake of clarity this book uses the terms "mentally handicapped" and "mentally disabled." However, it should be understood that I am not suggesting a mental state that is permanently unchanging. Except in cases of severe retardation, the mentally handicapped are slowed, not stopped.

Superstition. Dr. Charles Lee Feinberg, former dean of Talbot Theological Seminary, has noted that people "have for centuries viewed physical deficiencies and limitations in an altogether different light from those of a mental nature. The former have been met with sympathy and studied help, whereas the latter have almost universally received aversion, shame, and condemnation." As a result, in centuries past the mentally handicapped have been accused of being demon-possessed, specially cursed by evil spirits, and under divine judgment for the sins of their parents. These beliefs have led to the mentally handicapped being shunned, banished, and even killed by their communities.

Thankfully, scientific knowledge has led to increased human understanding. Most of us will no longer follow in the footsteps of ancestors who, because they believed the mentally handicapped were possessed or cursed, felt that harsh actions toward them—punishment and murder, for example—were justified. Still, even our enlightened twentieth century has seen the mentally handicapped being used—without their knowledge—in studies testing the effect in people of varying levels of radioactivity in food. If we believe that the mentally handicapped are simply healthy, mindless bodies, we can justify using their healthy tissue for science, and we can do so without worrying about getting anyone's permission. Similarly, if we believe the common superstition that the mentally handicapped are preoccupied with sexual thoughts—or if we believe that they have not earned the right to bear children—we can justify unauthorized sterilization and laws that prohibit marriage. The root philosophy seems to be the same in all of these cases: the mentally handicapped are not merely mentally debilitated, they are humanly something *less*.

Institutionalization. Institutions for the mentally handicapped serve a valuable role. For the severely disabled, they can provide the necessary, around-the-clock nursing care that no parent could hope to match. For those afflicted with conditions that could injure themselves or others, such places offer a safe, secure environment. For others, living in a home exclusively for the mentally handicapped can provide a helpful bridge between living with parents and living independently.

Institutions act as blinders, though, when they cause us—the general populace—to forget the people they serve. When the mentally handicapped attend special classes, travel together in special vans, and live in special places, we can overlook their presence in our society. Out of sight, out of mind. Rather than becoming common elements in our daily experience, they stand out as unusual, even odd. When we do encounter them—at the mall, at a ballgame, in church—we're likely to wonder what they're doing there. "Don't they belong in a 'home' somewhere?" we might wonder.

Obviously, some do. Murray Center, in my hometown of Centralia, Illinois, serves many people who would not find adequate care elsewhere. My sister lived there temporarily during her teen years, following what my parents describe as a nervous breakdown. But she was an unusual resident; most of the people there were and are far more severely handicapped than Barbara.

I remember visiting Murray with my father and standing beside the gurney-like bed of a profoundly disabled young man who will never walk, never form sentences, never feed himself, never even sit up. We were visiting him on behalf of the boy's father. A few days earlier the boy, momentarily unattended and free of his restraints, had rolled out of bed and fallen four feet to the hard linoleum floor, breaking his front teeth. His father, a minister and a friend of my father who lived several hours away, understandably was worried about him and asked Dad to check on him. I imagine he took me along for an education. It worked. The visit elicited strong feelings in me. I pitied the young man curled up on the gurney, mourning the stark division between my life and his, and stood there stunned by a loss he couldn't begin to comprehend. I grieved for his father as well. This was his beloved son, who could not register the father's presence or absence, who could not take his hand, who could not understand how deeply he shared his son's recent pain.

At the same time, I was grateful for two things: that this facility—and others like it across the country—exists, and that my sister no longer needed to be there. She had healed during her stay, and now she was where she was supposed to be—rubbing elbows with the world.

Fear. Nowadays many Christians sincerely wrestle with living out their faith in a world that is increasingly violent and uncertain. Do we stop to help a stranded motorist along the highway? Do we risk making eye contact with that panhandler in the subway? Who knows what actions such overtures might provoke? Some people have similar questions regarding the mentally handicapped. Perhaps they have been influenced by negative stereotypes in the media. Perhaps they have believed the myths of the mentally disabled having unusual strength or heightened sexual desire. Perhaps, too, they keep the mentally handicapped at bay because they fear what they represent: the fact that their handicap could just as easily have been our own or our child's; none of us has any guarantees, and that can be a frightening realization.

As Scripture tells us, "perfect love drives out fear" (1 John 4:18). And there is only one resource for "perfect love." When we see the mentally handicapped as God sees them, we can discover their true worth as human beings.

In *Look at Me, Please Look at Me*, author Dorothy Clark offered the following scenario:

I have a gift for you. Misshapen, torn . . . it is a large and cumbersome box. I place it in your hesitant hands. You smile as if to ask, "Is this a joke?" . . .

Slowly you lift the cover. A delightful fragrance emerges from the box. Pushing aside the layers of tissue you discover a bouquet of roses. They are deep red and just beginning to unfold.

Your face brightens. You lift the flowers. Inhale their perfume. Touch the cool, soft velvet petals.

"Thank you," your words tinged with wonder, leave an unspoken Why?

Had you rejected your gift because of the ugly wrapping, you would have missed the beauty of the real gift inside.

The mentally and physically handicapped are often like your package; difficult to look upon, unattractive, and in some instances even repulsive. But if you look past childlike minds and damaged bodies, you will discover God-created men, women, boys, and girls who are waiting to be wanted, to be accepted, to be loved.

You turn away, shaking your head. You say it is impossible to love and accept someone you normally would draw away from. You are right. But with Christ in you it is not impossible. He will accept and love them through you.

For me, replacing life's blinders with understanding means digging a bit deeper—into statistics, medical terminology, physiology.

Facts that can be scientifically verified help ground me in solid reality. Then I can begin to wrestle with the things science alone cannot clarify: How can we best serve the mentally handicapped? What are their deepest needs? Why are so many innocents so afflicted? What might God want for their lives? As I understand the roots of mental handicaps, my compassion for the mentally handicapped—along with my understanding of how my life fits alongside their own—deepens.

Perhaps some of the information that follows will be more than you want to know about mental handicaps; if so, sample what you need or want to know, then move on. The goal is not to become medical experts or social workers. Our goal is to equip ourselves to meet needy people on their own terms with the gospel of Jesus Christ.

THE FACTS ABOUT MENTAL HANDICAPS

In the United States alone, there are five to seven million mentally handicapped men and women, boys and girls. In worldwide terms, approximately three out of every hundred babies are born mentally handicapped, totalling 100,000-200,000 people annually.

Clinically speaking, to be mentally handicapped is to have an Intelligence Quotient, or IQ, below 70. (One hundred is considered "average," with "normal" falling anywhere between 85 and 115.) The large majority of the mentally handicapped, about 80 percent, are considered mildly handicapped, with IQs ranging from 55 to 70. The remaining 20 percent are designated moderate (IQ equals 40 to 54), severe (IQ equals 25 to 39), and profound (IQ equals 0 to 24). For some reason, more males than females are mentally handicapped. Some require constant medical care; others, like my sister, are able to live relatively normal lives with moderate supervision. Some battle physical disabilities, and some bear the physical characteristics of Down syndrome, or Mongolism.

It is difficult to pinpoint exact causes for mental handicaps because so many different factors may contribute to a

disability. However, the following list offers a brief introduction to several of the more significant reasons why mental handicaps occur.

Down syndrome. People with Down syndrome account
for a quarter of all the mentally handicapped. Also referred
to as Mongolism because it results in the flattened facial features and epicanthic folds similar to those of the Mongoloid
races (Eskimos, Polynesians, Chinese, etc.), Down syndrome is a congenital condition resulting from an extra
chromosome. Perhaps the most recognizable group among
the mentally handicapped, people with Down are often
openly affectionate and comfortable to be with. The bright,
smiling faces so typical in advertisements and promotions
for the mentally handicapped tend to be the faces of people
with Down syndrome.

Hydrocephalus. This condition results when cere-
brospinal fluid fails to drain properly from inside the skull,
building up until it saturates brain tissue, thus damaging it,
and actually enlarges the head. The causes of such build-up
include tumors, malformations that may occur in those with
spina bifida, and meningitis. Mental handicaps may be
avoided if the condition is promptly diagnosed and the
excess fluid is drained away.

PKU or phenylketonuria. PKU is a hereditary disor-
der that results in the lack of an enzyme needed to break
down and use phenylalanine, an amino acid present in all
foods with natural proteins. Most states now screen all
newborns for PKU within three days of birth via a blood
test; however, follow-up testing is often necessary for a reli-
able diagnosis.

While babies born with PKU will appear normal and
have normal intelligence, they inevitably will suffer brain
damage within three months if not placed on a restricted

diet. Such a diet, which may be required for many years, eliminates foods with phenylalanine, substituting others that will provide the nutrition necessary for normal development.

Rh disease (*also known as erythroblastosis fetalis and hemolytic disease*). About one out of every eight mothers will give birth to a child who will potentially bear Rh disease, a disease resulting from blood incompatibility between mother and child (the "Rh" designation coming from its initial discovery in the blood of Rhesus monkeys). While it kills approximately 6,000 babies each year, it handicaps about 20,000 others, with handicaps ranging from heart disease and hearing loss to mental disabilities. Recently a new drug has been introduced—Rh immune globulin—that dramatically reduces the dangers of Rh disease.

The disease itself is unusual, occurring only in women who are Rh-negative (approximately 10 to 15 percent of the female population). Instead of resulting from any defect or problem with either mother or child, it arises when an Rh-negative mother becomes pregnant with an Rh-positive child. When the child's Rh-positive blood interacts with the mother's, which happens most forcefully when the fetus is separated from the placenta (through birth, miscarriage, or abortion), the Rh factor enters the mother's bloodstream as a foreign substance; in some Rh-negative women, antibodies then form to fight it off as if it were an infection. While this situation poses little threat to the woman's first child, whose exit from the womb initiated the Rh changes, the subsequently formed antibodies will likely endanger future pregnancies, destroying or damaging any Rh-positive fetus.

An injection of Rh immune globulin has proven to be 99 percent effective in stopping the formation of the potentially dangerous antibodies when given to Rh-negative women within seventy-two hours of childbirth, miscarriage, or the abortion of their first child. However, the vaccine is temporary; it must be administered after each subsequent birth.

Rubella or German measles. Children whose mothers contracted rubella just prior to or during their pregnancy are at high risk for birth defects of many types. While fairly innocuous in children—causing a sore throat, a mild fever, and perhaps a slight rash for only several days—rubella can penetrate the womb of an expectant mother and seriously damage the growing fetus. For example, during a rubella epidemic in 1964 and 1965, more than 50,000 babies were stillborn or were born with hearing impairments, eye disorders, heart defects, and mental handicaps. Nowadays vaccinations of children, adolescent girls, and adult women help to eliminate the primary source of infection for pregnant women.

Birth defects. This is a general category encompassing the causes of mental handicaps not directly linked to genetics. Apart from the results of environmental pollutants (pesticides, pollution, chemical wastes), birth defects are largely a result of prenatal conditions. For example, poor nutrition, diabetes, hypertension, alcoholism, excessive exposure to X-rays, and certain drugs taken during the first trimester of pregnancy can all contribute to birth defects that may include mental handicaps. In addition, diseases contracted during pregnancy—rubella, genital herpes, toxoplasmosis, cytomegalovirus, and venereal disease—may lead to birth defects. Premature delivery also may cause problems. Lastly, many babies with birth defects are born to teenage mothers and mothers over the age of forty.

THE HARDEST QUESTION

Although I have touched only briefly on the medical causes for mental handicaps, no amount of scientific knowledge can answer the question likely to nag at us the most: Why? Not so much why did this happen—for about 85 percent of all cases, science can point to a likely cause—but why did it happen to us or to such nice people or to a family already so burdened? In short, why does God allow it?

I don't think I could answer that question any better than Dr. Maria Egg, a Swiss psychologist who did ground-breaking work with the mentally handicapped in the fifties and sixties. In her book *When a Child Is Different*, she says it perfectly:

> It seems that mental retardation is a part of Creation. For thousands of years we have known that there are mentally retarded people in the world. . . . It is probably as old as the human race. From this we might well conclude that this condition, too, has its purpose— even though we may not be able to grasp the sense of it in each particular case.
>
> Some parents think that God gave them a retarded child as a punishment because they are not good people. It is generally the deeply religious who have this reaction. But this is not according to what the Bible says. The Gospel of St. John relates that two thousand years ago the Apostles asked Jesus the same question countless parents are still asking Him today. ["His disciples asked him, 'Rabbi, who sinned, this man or his parents, that he was born blind?' 'Neither this man nor his parents sinned,' said Jesus, 'but this happened so that the work of God might be displayed in his life,'" John 9:2-3]
>
> Let all fathers and mothers of retarded children inscribe this sentence in their hearts, for it tells us that this child was not given by way of punishment and that his existence is in keeping with divine law.

Obviously, not all parents will see the hand of God at work in their lives through their mentally handicapped children. In fact, I have seen a videotape of a frail-looking, seventy-year-old mother of a mentally disabled man who told the interviewer she would never wish such a curse on anyone. The sag of her shoulders and the tired resignation in her voice were evidence that she meant it. In her eyes, her son was a daily reminder that she had failed as a mother; his presence told the world she was not perfect.

SURPRISED BY MY FATHER'S LOVE

I have never considered my sister to be a "curse," but as a teenager I wrestled with my own feelings of resentment and anger toward her. It took a terrible accident to shake me up enough to question those feelings and to come to the kind of deeper understanding that led to the research and writing of this book.

The accident occurred about nine years ago, when Barbara was walking home from her job at the sheltered workshop. There, she and her friends make brooms and fishing lures, help recycle aluminum cans and newspapers, and do a host of other "contract work." Those who can only count to five are assigned piecework of five or fewer pieces. Those who can do nothing else are taught basic grooming skills. At the time, Barbara was doing well at her job and was able to function with little supervision and was enjoying daily contact with friends, some of whom she had known for more than a dozen years.

One Thursday, late in the afternoon, she walked to a four-stop intersection, streets she had crossed umpteen times before. I imagine that her fear of cars probably caused her to hesitate and look both ways while still safely on the curb. Then she stepped into the street, her head down as always.

A light-blue pickup truck, its driver blinded by the glare of a brilliant sunset, ran its stop sign and skidded around the corner. The front bumper caught Barbara hard at the thighs, knocking her to the pavement and sending her glasses through the air. The truck rolled on for several yards, then slammed to a stop. The driver threw open his cab door and ran back to my sister, now lying in the street.

Barbara lay semi-conscious in a growing puddle of blood. As I learned later, her eyes already showed signs of bruising as dark-hued rings blossomed against her suddenly pale skin. Her throat began to swell, and she gasped for air, fighting back the clot rising in her throat.

Both sets of tires had rolled directly over her stomach. The driver, a seventeen-year-old with no insurance, tore off his shirt, rolled it into a ball, and placed it under her head. He ran across the street to a corner gas station and telephoned for an ambulance.

I learned of the accident when my mother called me at my apartment in Woodridge, Illinois, some 200 miles from Centralia, where my parents and Barbara lived. I was stunned. By what miracle had Barbara survived? The story just didn't make sense to me. And sense didn't come as I mulled over the events during my six-hour drive to southern Illinois. The only solid thought to come out of it was, "Why?" Why Barbara? Why now—when she was enjoying her job, making progress with a new doctor (to this day Barbara's doctors are constantly varying her medications and dosages), and hopeful for the future?

What happened subsequently has gotten tangled up a bit in my mind. The intervening years, the emotional nature of the event, and my own published "fictionalized" account have led to memories I'm not sure are based on what actually happened. However, the following is what I remember. While the details may be hazy, my impressions—and the results they led to—are what seem most important.

My parents were at Barbara's bedside when I arrived. Mom was standing to her left, carefully running a brush through Barbara's unwashed waves of hair. Dad stood across from her, his back to the door, holding Barbara's pale hand tightly in his own. He turned to me with a tired smile.

When I looked down at my sister, my first feeling was anger. Her puffed face was mottled with blackened bruises. Her eyes were nearly swollen shut. Tiny flecks of dried blood were still caked in the corners of her mouth. Thin tubes dangled from both arms and led to bottles hanging nearby on metal stalks.

"Hi, brother," Barbara said hoarsely. She made a futile attempt to open her eyes a little wider.

I smiled and swallowed hard. "How are you feeling?" I asked, hoping she felt better than she looked. It was only a simple question, nothing taxing. But Barbara often doesn't like being asked questions, even simple ones, even when they come from her little brother. She didn't answer. For several minutes she was very quiet. Then she slowly turned to face Dad and said—so faintly I almost thought I imagined it—"I love you, Dad."

Dad, still holding her hand, looked genuinely surprised. Not so much at the words—Barbara often told him she loved him—but at their coming at that moment, I think. Soon calm spread across his face. A tenderness I didn't think I'd ever seen before brought tears to his eyes. The truth was obvious: Dad loved Barbara back. Knowing that made me reflect on my own feelings. But just when I wanted to feel supportive and caring as far as Barbara was concerned, I realized that the emotions welling up inside me didn't have much to do with brotherly love.

I remembered the embarrassment I felt in grade school when my friends came over to play, only to discover that I had a mentally handicapped older sister who wanted to join in. I remembered the faces of a few of my mother's "concerned friends" at church, the ones who asked if Barbara had ever been to a doctor. And I remembered my own jealousy whenever she received more attention than I did.

That was only the tip of the iceberg. The more I thought about my life with Barbara, the more frustrated I became with what I saw. I recalled the night I came home from a date and begged my parents to adopt a "normal" sister for me (ignoring the fact that my parents were a couple in their mid-fifties with two children ages twenty-four and fourteen). I wanted a sister who could stay up late to give me advice, tell me what it might feel like to be fresh out of college and hopelessly unemployed, get married and make me a proud and happy uncle. It was always painfully clear to me that Barbara would not be that sister—could never be, no matter what.

Dad's attitude has always impressed me, though. Throughout Barbara's life he has known that she is someone special. She was created, he would say, to be loved—and loved wholeheartedly. Whenever he scolded her for some bad habit, tickled her with a day's worth of beard stubble, or quoted Bible verses to her, he was telling her that she was someone precious in God's sight. He made it plain that an important part of him would die if he ever lost her. His example gave me much to consider during the next tense days of waiting as Barbara began to heal.

The following week Barbara was released from the hospital. Miraculously, she had suffered no broken bones, no ruptured organs. Even so, she was sore, and her movements were a little slower than usual. There was an even worse downside: the experience brought on a terrible mental setback. Soon it became clear that Barbara could no longer live in her apartment alone. After placing their hope in the promise of independent living, my parents found themselves searching for other forms of care for my sister. One awful afternoon accident left ripples that would last literally for years.

Several months later, while clearing out an old dresser drawer, I came across a childhood photo album. As I turned the thick, yellowed pages of cellophane and watched my life unfold, I couldn't help taking a personal inventory, evaluating my past and wondering about my future. One picture practically jumped off the page.

It was an informal black-and-white family photograph taken on my first birthday. All eyes are focused on me; it is my day for glory. Mom, beaming, is proudly holding me on her lap, steadying my uncertain torso with both hands. Barbara is a bright-eyed eleven-year-old sitting to Mom's right.

Dad is standing behind, to Mom's left. The look of fatherly love that had swept across his face at the hospital— the look I didn't think I had ever seen before—is captured forever in that photograph. That was the smile he had displayed when Barbara had told him she loved him. It had meant he loved her just as much. Now, here, it seemed that he loved me in the identical way. It wasn't a love given because I had accomplished anything great, showed wonderful potential, or had a "normal" brain. He loved me like he loved Barbara: simply for being his child. He loved me with God's own love.

At that moment I began to understand something of my

father's compassion for my sister and for the mentally hand-icapped in general. It is unconditional and all-encompass-ing—a love that sees the heart and the soul rather than the IQ chart. That is the kind of love that can flourish as we get to know and minister to the mentally handicapped. If this book can help to nurture that, it will have served its purpose.

Chapter 2

FROM MYTHS TO
MINISTRY

*If I speak in the tongues of men and of angels, but have not love,
I am only a resounding gong or a clanging cymbal. If I have the
gift of prophecy and can fathom all mysteries and all knowledge,
and if I have a faith that can move mountains, but have not love,
I am nothing. If I give all I possess to the poor and surrender my
body to the flames, but have not love, I gain nothing.
Love is patient, love is kind. It does not envy, it does not boast,
it is not proud. It is not rude, it is not self-seeking, it is not easily
angered, it keeps no record of wrongs. Love does not delight in
evil but rejoices with the truth.*

1 CORINTHIANS 13:1-6

We have nine mentally handicapped people who attend
our services."

"Three mentally disabled young people come to our
Sunday school."

"There's a group home for the mentally handicapped
just down the block, and they bring as many of their people
as they can on Sunday morning."

"When we got up to half a dozen, we decided to start a
special Sunday school class for the mentally disabled."

"We lead only a small congregation, but we're eager to

get started in this kind of outreach. We've done it in the past and found it extremely fulfilling."

"The mother of a mentally handicapped young man in our church decided that her son needed a special class, so she started one. One year later, we have five regular students."

"All of the mentally handicapped members have specific responsibilities within the church. That's the only way to let them know we love and trust them. Besides, it builds their self-esteem to have useful work."

"Our mentally disabled Sunday school class visits a nursing home once a month to cheer up the elderly people there. I think it's safe to say *everyone* loves it."

Today a number of churches big and small are actively reaching out to the spiritual, social, and physical needs of the mentally handicapped. These churches have taken it on themselves to exemplify the patience, kindness, and humility needed to work effectively with the mentally disabled. And love is the reason.

That has not always been the case. Religious people have not always been capable of seeing their own humanity in the faces of their mentally handicapped sisters and brothers. In fact, historically the church's response to the mentally disabled has swung widely between the poles of quiet acceptance and utter denial of their personhood. While this chapter can touch only lightly on a very few of the major views and significant figures seen in the history of mental handicaps, I believe that even a "nutshell" understanding of how these responses changed, matured, and expanded over time can help us better understand our roles with the mentally handicapped today—in the enlightened 1990s.

MYTHS, FOOLS, AND THE POSSESSED

One writer has noted that it is reasonable to believe that for as long as humanity has walked the earth there likely have been cases of mental handicaps. But except for a few minor hints in Greek and Roman literature, there is very little from the ancient world that can be directly linked with the presence or treatment of the mentally disabled. Assumptions have been drawn from the barest facts. And the stories that have been passed down often have the hollow ring of apocrypha.

For instance, some have suggested that St. Nicholas Thaumaturges, the fourth-century Bishop of Myra who has passed into folklore as *the* St. Nicholas, was also supposedly well-known for his protection of the feeble-minded. However, next to nothing is really known of his life or ministry, and there is no way to substantiate his views of the mentally handicapped or what, if any, actions he took on their behalf. (Consider that Nicholas has also been dubbed the patron saint of children, sailors, and pawnbrokers!) There is also the lingering legend of a woman named Euphrasia from Constantinople who, following her husband's death, gave away her possessions, moved to the family estate in Egypt, and lived as a nun, looking after the homeless and the mentally disabled.

If this were our sole understanding of the ancients' reaction to mental handicaps, we might assume that everyone looked on them with almost fairy-tale kindness. Unfortunately, that is not the case. The plight of the mentally handicapped in the ancient world was not a happy one.

In Rome, the mentally disabled were often kept as household "fools" or jesters, who were responsible for providing entertainment for the family and guests. Although

41

some became well-known to the point of having official biographers, it is reasonable to assume that many endured an existence similar to the one described in a letter by the first-century Roman Stoic philosopher Seneca:

> You know that Herpaste, my wife's fool, was left on my hands as a hereditary charge, for I have a natural aversion to these monsters; and if I have a mind to laugh at a fool, I need not seek him far, I can laugh at myself. This fool has suddenly lost her sight. I am telling you a strange but true story. She is not aware that she is blind and constantly urges her keeper to take her out because she says my house is dark.

By the fifteenth century, it was clear that even Christians were not immune to the prevailing disregard of the mentally handicapped. Here is commentary from one of Christianity's most significant figures:

> Eight years ago, there was one at Dessau whom I, Martin Luther, saw and grappled with. He was twelve years old, had the use of his eyes and all his senses, so that one might think that he was a normal child. But he did nothing but gorge himself as much as four peasants or threshers. He ate, defecated and drooled and . . . screamed. If things didn't go well, he wept. So I said to the Prince of Anhalt: "If I were the Prince, I should take this child to the Moldau River which flows near Dessau and drown him." But the Prince of Anhalt . . . refused to follow my advice. . . .

According to one historian, "When Luther was asked why he had made such a recommendation he replied that he was firmly of the opinion that such changelings were merely a mass of flesh, a *massa carnis*, with no soul. 'For it is in the Devil's power that he corrupts people who have reason and souls when he possesses them. The Devil sits in such changelings where their soul should have been!'"

Of course, we can certainly wonder whether the church's great reformer truly witnessed demonic activity. But we can also reasonably ask, as several authorities have suggested, whether he simply met someone who was mentally handicapped. It is impossible to know for sure. But if it was the latter case, his reasoning was not out of step with other respected people in his day.

An alternate but equally inaccurate attitude—though one not any less humorous for its fallacy—arose among a small part of the European scientific community in the late 1500s. Led by Danish astronomer Tycho Brahe, these people of science believed that all the spoken words of the mentally handicapped were divinely inspired. So they followed them wherever they walked, dutifully scribbling down every word that passed through their lips and following their pronouncements to the best of their ability. Elsewhere, some who kept household "fools" believed that their "foolishness" was a special mark from God. This mistaken belief actually had a positive result for those in their care: these owners chose not to beat or mock their charges.

Today these attitudes sound foolish and hopelessly mired in the wrong-headed thinking of past, ignorant generations. Yet it is difficult to blame the so-called normal people of history who simply did not know any better. They *couldn't* know any better, for there was practically no medical research of mental handicaps that could prove the mentally disabled weren't demon-possessed or soulless, inhuman masses of flesh. The scientific community could not have cared less about the affliction. That would not change significantly until the eighteenth century, when a man named Jacob Rodriguez Pereire put forth a radical new theory.

GROUNDBREAKING WORK

The first groups organized specifically to care for the mentally handicapped sprang up in the early 1800s, largely inspired by the groundbreaking example of Giacobo (Jacob) Rodriguez Pereire (1715-1780), a man remembered today as the father of physiological education for his groundbreaking work with the deaf and mute. The surprising theory of his that drew worldwide attention—not to mention its share of ridicule and skepticism—was this: that people who were deaf and mute could learn to communicate. Prior to Pereire, such people were considered utterly hopeless.

Born in Portugal, the Jewish Pereire left his homeland for France due to religious persecution. There he is said to have met and fallen in love with a girl who had been unable to speak from birth. For her sake, he devoted himself to discovering a way to give her the gift of speech. The result was a single-handed sign language that proved to the world what he already knew in his heart: that the deaf and mute *could* learn to communicate. He went on to work personally with a deaf teenage boy of a noble family, eventually drawing the attention of King Louis XV, who honored him with a pension. Soon he had established a private school for the deaf. In 1760 Pereire's persistence—not to mention his love that first set him on his quest—helped to earn him a membership in the Royal Society of London.

Although Pereire's work was not focused primarily on the mentally handicapped, the implications for the education of such persons were immediately seen by his contemporaries.

One who eventually put those implications to the test was Jean Marie Gaspard Itard (1774-1838), physician at the School for Deaf-Mutes in Paris, who devoted five years of his life trying to teach and civilize a mentally handicapped boy of eleven or twelve who had been found living in the wild. A famous psychologist of the day had declared the boy "an incurable idiot, inferior to domestic animals." Itard thought differently. Although he was young (then only twenty-five) and relatively inexperienced, he was convinced that the boy's mental deficiencies had been compounded by social and educational neglect. By making improvements in the boy's social development, he believed it might be possible to make strides toward improving the boy's mental abilities as well.

Ultimately, Itard was unsuccessful in leading the boy from, as he wrote, "savagery to civilization." But while he failed to please himself, his years of work made a remarkable impact on his peers. After all, the boy, who had been named Victor, had come to Itard mute, walking on all fours, and violent toward anything that got in his way. After five years, Victor could recognize different letters in the alphabet, understand a limited vocabulary, and name objects. Although Itard's results fell short of his goals, the French Academy of Science pronounced his progress "astonishing." The Academy then went on to make a comment that is still valuable for us today. They wrote: "To appreciate the real worth of [Itard's] labors, the pupil ought to be compared only with himself; we should remember what he was when placed in the hands of his physician, see what he is now, and more, consider the distance separating his starting point from that which he has reached."

Itard succeeded alone, without anyone waiting in the wings to pick up on his work and move it to the next stage. In fact, another major event in the care of the mentally handicapped child would not capture the world's attention until after his death.

It began in 1836, when a young, charismatic Swiss physician named Johann Jakob Guggenbühl (1816-1863) heard a recitation of the Lord's Prayer that changed the course of his life and led him to establish methods of caring for the mentally handicapped that continue today. But what Guggenbühl began as a glorious experiment was destined to end far differently.

SAVIOR OR CHARLATAN?

Were Guggenbühl alive today, the story of his life's work might begin with write-ups in various respected journals of science and medicine, proceed to the inspirational, Christian-toned *Guideposts*, eventually branch out to popular readers through *Time* and *Newsweek*, move on to the less-newsy *People*, and wind up shouting at us from the cover of the *National Enquirer* at the local grocery store. A cheesy TV movie-of-the-week would follow, putting the final nail in the coffin of his reputation and reminding every viewer that good intentions alone are not always enough when trying to meet the needs of the mentally handicapped.

Guggenbühl was twenty years old when he first encountered a mentally disabled person. While traveling through the village of Seedorf, he came upon a man he described as a "dwarfed, crippled cretin of stupid appearance" who was mumbling his way through the Lord's Prayer at a wayside cross. His spirit touched by the man's simple piety, Guggenbühl followed him home. There the physician learned that the man's mother had taught him the prayer during childhood. Ever since, he had made a point of praying it at the cross at the same time every day, rain or shine. Unfortunately, the mother and son were very poor, and she could afford no formal education for her boy. Guggenbühl had an idea.

The fact that the boy had learned a prayer, and had developed the habit of faithfully praying it, led the physician to change his mind regarding the educability of the mentally handicapped. For despite Itard's inroads, common wisdom still said that "idiotic children" were utterly incapable of learning or developing mentally. Yet this boy's example argued against such wisdom. He *had* learned. And Guggenbühl could not help wondering how much more the boy might have learned had his mother been blessed with the resources to teach him.

At the time there were no institutions that truly cared for the mentally handicapped. The places that were available to them were prison-like institutions and workhouses, places that made no attempt whatsoever to educate or train. There was no place in the world devoted to the medical care of the mentally handicapped. Guggenbühl vowed to change that, believing that God was calling him to be an avenue through which the mentally disabled might be served.

Guggenbühl founded his institution, called Abendberg, in 1842 on forty acres of donated land near Interlaken, on a mountain summit. Its credo was: "The immortal soul is essentially the same in every creature born of woman." This was an idea as strange and unprecedented as Pereire's assertion that the deaf and mute were able to learn to communicate. It became a clarion call that, along with the pragmatic, day-to-day care provided by a group known as the Evangelical Sisters of Mercy, served Guggenbühl well. His institution was an immediate success, drawing praise and admiring visitors from around the world. Inspired by his model, praiseworthy facilities were soon established in

Germany, Austria, Great Britain, the Netherlands, Scandinavia, and the United States.

One contemporary wrote of Abendberg in glowing terms:

> [Guggenbühl] employed a Sister of Mercy for every three pupils, besides having a skilled male teacher. Idiots require to be taught cleanly in their habits, to wash and dress themselves, to use a spoon, and afterwards a knife and fork. Speech has to be evoked or improved, their senses to be aroused, the use of their limbs, and especially the use of their fingers to be developed; their faculties of attention and imitation to be cultivated; elementary instruction to be imparted in an interesting manner, without producing weariness, the teacher's mind dropping, as it were, into the minds of the pupils; good manners have to be engendered and bad habits counteracted. Their confidence has to be won by kindness, and then their wills can be guided by tact and firmness; their moral and religious sense has to be awakened, and some Scriptural knowledge to be conveyed, so as to excite, with God's help, simple faith in Him as their Father, Jesus as their Saviour, and heaven as their home.

To many, this was exactly the approach needed to bring some sense of normality to the lives of the mentally handicapped. But trouble was brewing. Abendberg had caught the attention of the world, and the world's expectations of Guggenbühl's new project grew impossibly high. Thanks in part to Guggenbühl's own penchant for telling his bankers and supporters whatever he felt they wanted to hear, Abendberg was not only expected to train and to teach the mentally disabled but to cure them as well. That simply was not possible. The solution, in Guggenbühl's mind, was a series of "white lies" that moved from being unethical to engaging in downright fraud. For example, to please his admirers he eventually filled one-third of Abendberg with normal people and passed them off as formerly mentally handicapped citizens who were now cured. But as his claims for his community increased, so did public scrutiny. Such a charade could not stand up to the critical probes that followed, and Abendberg was closed amid charges of gross mismanagement and outright misrepresentation.

Ironically, as Abendberg was forced to send its residents packing and shut its doors in the midst of scandal, the institutions that had modeled themselves on Abendberg were flourishing around the world. There was a need for their work, and God was blessing it.

THE GOOD WORK OF THE CHURCH

Prior to Abendberg, homes for the mentally handicapped were limited to asylums associated with hospitals or churches. A Benedictine monastery in Admont, Styria (a district in Austria) cared for twelve mentally handicapped people until a fire, tragically set by a resident, burned it to the ground in 1865. Also, a pastor in Würtemberg, Germany, took a number of mentally handicapped children into his own home, caring for them for twelve years until a lack of support from his parishioners forced him to find a new home for them. Fortunately, a new institution in Marieberg, the first to be established by a government, was opening and was willing to take the children in.

In France, a musician, horse lover, and soldier turned to God and became an ordained minister. Jean Bost went on to found an orphanage with seventy-five normal and healthy young girls. When two mentally handicapped children showed up on his doorstep, Bost concluded that they might not be comfortable with the others, so he took them home to live with him. In 1855 he established a special home for the mentally handicapped, which he named Bethesda, starting with five girls. In 1858, he founded Shiloh, a similar home for boys.

In the United States, however, outreach to the mentally handicapped has taken a different path.

Institutional care formally began with Samuel Gridley Howe (1801-1876), a graduate of Harvard Medical School, whose interest in helping the blind and the insane carried over to his work with the mentally handicapped. Forty years after he opened his first institution in Massachusetts, fifteen more facilities opened.

Howe provides an interesting bridge between Europe and America in terms of work with the mentally handicapped. While Europe's training schools, asylums, homes, and institutions for the mentally disabled were founded by spiritual leaders—who had little or no formal medical training— nearly every one of their counterparts in the United States was founded by professional physicians who came to their task with no spiritual agenda. Howe, however, was medically trained but was also apparently a firm believer in the power of God. As one biographer has written, "Probably no person in the history of the United States was more concerned about people in need, more effective in realizing appropriate programs for them, or more personally sacrificing."

CHANGING TIMES

Perhaps it was the echoes of the scandal at Abendberg, which had been associated from the outset with the "divine call of God." Perhaps the medically oriented U.S. facilities established by Howe had begun to catch the world's attention. Perhaps it was the global shift of modernity, which encouraged an abandonment of the old—things religious—in favor of the new—things scientific and quantifiable. Whatever the case, as the 1800s drew to a close, around the globe a specifically Christian response to mental handicaps was becoming harder and harder to find.

Not that dedicated Christians were not at work. One significant crusader was Pastor Martin Heinrich Sengelmann of Germany. His passion was educating children. After establishing himself with a successful vocational school in 1850, he opened an asylum for the mentally handicapped in 1863. He then took on a grand task: the establishment of a triennial conference of directors of German institutions for the mentally disabled.

It would not be accurate to say that his first conference was an unqualified success. Because of his own religious leanings, Pastor Sengelmann was adamant that a Christian worldview dominate the proceedings. And dominate it did. With speakers made up largely of theologians and Christian educators, the conference emphasized the importance of prayer as a "cure" for mental handicaps and held up, as the primary goal, the instilling of Christian character. A panel met to debate whether the mentally handicapped should be confirmed into the church. Not surprisingly, many of those in attendance, who did not share Sengelmann's agenda, were frustrated by the spiritual focus.

It is interesting how the actions of people who responded to the mentally disabled in the most common-sensical way possible were viewed as being utterly unenlightened to many in the late 1800s. When Jean Bost met two mentally handicapped girls who he did not think would be happy in his orphanage, he took them home. When there were no homes for the mentally disabled in Würtemberg, a pastor opened his home for twelve years. Simple as that. And the one climactic idea that arose from the first conference sponsored by Pastor Sengelmann reflected what these earlier caregivers had known from the start: not every mentally handicapped child belongs in an institution.

To sum up the early years of professional interest in the mentally handicapped, historian Leo Kanner offers these words in his enlightening study *A History of the Care and Study of the Mentally Retarded*:

> In brief, the care and study of the mentally retarded had its origin as a *philanthropic* enterprise intended to "cure" severely defective persons in residential settings. This was shared by a few physicians, many educators (especially teachers of deaf-mutes), and dedicated clergymen. The introduction of special classes put the major task into the hands of *educators*. Eventually *psychologists* entered the field in search of reliable criteria for the evaluation of intellectual endowment. Thus philanthropy, education, and psychology were the consecutive godfathers of progress.
>
> This was the state of affairs by 1910. All efforts were bent on doing something for the betterment of the lot and functioning of mentally retarded individuals.

But that state of affairs changed radically in 1910, when public favor turned against the mentally handicapped.

The change had been hinted at for a number of years. In 1865 a Sir Francis Galton intimated that the future of the human race was endangered by the intermarriage and procreation of the mentally handicapped. In 1877 a penologist named Dugdale published a genealogical study of the Jukes family, a family of questionable intelligence whose history of intermarriage had resulted in a long line of paupers and a majority of descendants who were of "low physical and moral standard."

Fourteen years later Rev. O. C. McCulloch presented a speech at an annual session of the National Conference of Charities and Correction that supported Dugdale's findings with biblical references to the "tribe of Ishmael." His solution to maintaining the purity of the human race was three-fold: cease outpatient assistance; keep private assistance to such individuals in check; and "get hold of the children." When Dugdale's book, perhaps not coincidentally, was reprinted in 1910, it found great favor with its underscoring of the growing apprehension about the place of the mentally handicapped in society.

That apprehension reached its peak with the widely publicized accounts of the pseudonymously named "Kallikak" family, a family whose lineage was proved to have been "corrupted" over a half-dozen generations by an illicit liaison between a normal man and a mentally handicapped woman. By following the two lines of the Kallikaks—normal and "feebleminded"—social scientists presented what seemed like incontrovertible evidence of the danger of procreation among the mentally handicapped.

> From [Martin Kallikak] have come 480 descendants; 143 of these, we have conclusive proof were or are fee-bleminded while only forty-six have been found normal. . . . Among these 480 descendants, thirty-six have been illegitimate; there have been thirty-three sexually immoral persons, mostly prostitutes; there have been twenty-four confirmed alcoholics; there have been three epileptics; eighty-two died in infancy; three were criminals; eight kept houses of ill fame.

When Martin eventually straightened up and married a "respectable girl of good family," the results seemed to take on an entirely different character.

> All of the legitimate children . . . married into the best families in their state, the descendents of colonial governors, signers of the Declaration of Independence, soldiers, and even the founders of a great university. . . . There are doctors, lawyers, judges, educators, traders, landholders, in short, respectable citizens, men and women prominent in every phase of social life.

The results seemed obvious: "Feeblemindedness is hereditary and transmitted as surely as any other character." Not that there weren't objections to these conclusions. But the voices of the rational minority were increasingly overwhelmed by a flurry of reports from the field that gave credence to those who feared the increase of the mentally handicapped. This so-called eugenics scare reached its zenith—or, perhaps, its nadir—when a special committee of the American Breeders' Association announced possible responses to the problem in 1911:

1. Do nothing and the problem will disappear
2. Euthanasia
3. Restrictive marriage laws
4. Education (training the retarded not to intermarry)
5. Proscribed systems of matings, to remove defective traits
6. Scientific breeding
7. Birth control
8. Environmental improvement
9. Institutionalization
10. Sterilization

Although study into mental handicaps has never suffered a complete breakdown, it is fair to say that this new fear of the mentally handicapped ushered in a twenty-four-year "dark age."

THE CHURCH AND THE MENTALLY HANDICAPPED FROM 1910 TO THE PRESENT

From an official, professional point of view, the church ceased to be a groundbreaking force in the care of the mentally handicapped during those twenty-four years, succumbing at last to the death throes that had begun with the collapse of Abendberg during the previous century. The innovations and enthusiasm that would soon return in regard to the mentally disabled would be the fruits of science, not faith.

Enthusiasm was sparked in 1934 when a Norwegian scientist named Dr. Ivar Folling discovered phenylketonuria, the chemical responsible for a metabolic disturbance that played a major role in mental handicaps at that time. Not only did he find a cause, he found the cure: proper diet. His findings inaugurated a new era of enlightened research and increased understanding of the mentally handicapped.

Subsequent years saw increasing scientific interest in the causes of mental handicaps, specifically in relationship to work concerning human chromosomes.

Yet, two highly significant social leaps for the mentally handicapped got their start in 1950 and 1963 respectively. In 1950 a group formed calling itself the National Association for Retarded Children; within ten years it had grown to include 50,000 parents and friends of the mentally handicapped. Today, it is known as the Association for Retarded Citizens (ARC) and has grown into a significant political lobbying body representing well over 100,000 members. The second event occurred in 1963 when

President John F. Kennedy established the President's Panel on Mental Retardation to study and combat mental handicaps. The efforts of these two groups, along with continuing advances in sociology, psychology, psychiatry, and medicine, have provided the mentally disabled with the most positive, productive environment in history.

As a result of these two events, a number of Christians who were counseling or supervising the mentally handicapped—or who had given birth to and raised brain-damaged children—published a flurry of books in the fifties and sixties about the Christian's response to the mentally disabled, some staying in print for a decade or more. Although these books broke little new scientific ground, they went a long way toward establishing a more open and loving attitude toward the mentally handicapped. They were willing to acknowledge the humanity and the neediness of the mentally disabled, and they viewed outreach and loving acceptance as the natural outgrowth of Christian faith.

Thanks to these advances in science and social acceptance, many mentally handicapped adults can now live in independent situations, hold regular jobs alongside normal coworkers, attend classes tailored to their needs and educational level, receive counseling, and marry and have families.

Still, despite these advances, it is not unusual for the spiritual needs of the mentally handicapped to go unrecognized and unmet. And while churches may yearn to reach out to them, many cannot recognize the need, or they wonder where to begin, worry about discipline and training, puzzle over curriculum choices, and debate the question of whether or not to integrate the mentally disabled with their normal peers.

Ministering to the mentally handicapped is not an easy task. But it is being done with wonderful results in churches and homes across the country. The following chapters explore how some Christians today are reaching out to this underserved group—and how you can too.

Chapter 3

THE SPIRITUAL NEEDS
OF THE MENTALLY HANDICAPPED

In his book *The Lambs of Libertyville*, author Tim Unsworth describes a community of mentally handicapped citizens established on a farm in Libertyville, Illinois. Begun by Bob Terese and Corinne Owen, members of Wheaton (IL) Baptist Church, Lamb's Farm is a commercial venture staffed entirely by mentally disabled women and men, many of them "on-campus" residents. Lamb's Farm is located beside a busy Chicago expressway, and it features a restaurant, gift and craft shops, and even a small working farm. It is, remarkably, a success. But it did not happen overnight. It took years of trial and error; of discovering how to link workers with the jobs that would challenge and inspire them— with minimal stress and frustration; of learning when to let go and to look on as the young people acquired the skills necessary to leave the shelter of the farm and take part in the world at large.

Through Lamb's Farm, Bob and Corinne have helped train literally hundreds of mentally handicapped individuals. In the process they received a training of their own. But perhaps the most important information they gained was also the most basic and the most important for all who work with—or desire to work with—the mentally disabled. "They're just like us," Bob Terese learned. "It's really simple. They are simply ordinary people with special problems. We're all the same. It's simply that we have different levels of understanding."

Unfortunately, Bob's level of understanding, at least as it relates to the mentally handicapped, is not always shared wholeheartedly among modern church members. Despite the long history of Christian involvement in the lives, education, and training of the mentally handicapped, despite the continuing increase in public awareness of the mentally disabled in daily life, and despite legislation and social organizations that work actively toward the goal that all disabled people should be treated with equanimity—despite all of these things, many in the church today are still uncertain of what, if anything, we should be doing to help the mentally handicapped.

I discovered one of the clearest, most succinct reasons for Christian involvement with the mentally handicapped in Sigurd Petersen's book *Retarded Children: God's Children*, now long out of print.

> A theology that makes one comfortable with retarded people issues from the Biblical doctrine that man has been created in the image of God, that he is redeemed by Christ, that he is immortal, and that in the eternal life promised by God all imperfection shall be corrected in the fulfillment of the individual's capacities and destiny according to the purpose of God. This makes human life precious, something to be handled with care, to be nurtured to its highest capacities for usefulness and happiness. The retarded should, therefore, be loved for Christ's sake, and on his behalf.

But Petersen goes on to wrestle with the Christian's desire to reach out in love and with the fact that damaged people have been born into God's world.

> The stark reality of retardation, the fact that something happens to children that limits them for life, forces us to ask why this must be. It is, of course, only one of many questions involving suffering, sorrow, and evil. To say that this is all God's will would not be Christ's answer, nor would it resolve the problem. Neither must we say it is the consequence of sin. In some cases it might be, but certainly it is far from being a complete answer. We must begin by saying that since human life is not a mechanical thing, but a living process, it is subject to variations. There are physical laws at work in conception, heredity, growth, injury, etc., to which human life is subjected. Involved in all these factors in life is man's consciousness, which takes recognition of and adds meaning to what happens. Since man adds meaning, and therefore values, to all that happens, suffering becomes a spiritual or religious problem. . . . There is evil in the world and in us, and that suffering can easily be associated with our sense of guilt.

THE CHURCH'S RESPONSE

One way I gathered information for this book was through a random survey distributed to approximately 200 churches in the United States. My mailing list included small churches and large, rural and urban, long-established and two years old. Given the variety of churches surveyed, I was surprised by the similar tone among churches that reported having had no experience with ministering to the mentally handicapped. I can only describe their responses as resignedly complacent or guardedly hopeful:

"As the opportunity arises and time and resources permit, I'd like to see a ministry developed among the mentally handicapped."

"We don't target the mentally disabled as a group."

"The issue of ministry to particular constituencies is just now emerging."

"We are a small church and have not grown to the point where we have the facilities, resources, or personnel to target this group."

"Three or four just attend church. We are not having an outreach there."

"Four attend church; two are members. But we currently have no active outreach to the mentally handicapped. No one has pressed for a ministry to this group."

"In my last parish the local institution sent a few individuals to our worship services."

"The only mentally handicapped person [in our church] attends services, as our theology emphasizes worship. However, beyond that there is nothing for the girl."

"There is not much interest in our church in doing anything special for the two mentally disabled people who attend."

Perhaps I would not have found these answers so discouraging if it weren't for the answers supplied by a number of other churches—churches similar in congregation size, type of community, budget, and so on. These churches described: new ministries to the mentally handicapped that were flourishing, mentally disabled members who were playing an active part in weekly worship and in small groups, congregations whose faith was being deepened because of the spiritual changes they were witnessing among the mentally handicapped in their midst.

The first, more quietly pessimistic group of churches seemed to be holding back, missing out on something good. (This seems particularly the case in those churches that had mentally handicapped members and visitors but had no plans to serve their special needs in any specific way.)

As a freelance writer and a former book editor, I find it not uncommon to meet up with people who talk about the book they'd "like to write someday, if I just had the time." They have wonderful stories to tell, they say; they just don't have the time to commit them to paper. There also are folks who say they'd love to write, but they haven't yet decided whether they should use that battered old Royal typewriter they inherited from a great-uncle, purchase an inexpensive word processor, or make the leap to a full-fledged computer; they need to get some more advice before they can make their decision and get down to the actual work of writing.

When a young wanna-be writer asked author Annie Dillard, who won the Pulitzer Prize for her nonfiction book *A Pilgrim at Tinker Creek*, whether she thought he had what it took to be a successful author, Dillard said to him, "I don't know; do you like sentences?" The young man looked back at her quizzically. Her point was that talent, best sellers, knowledge of the classics, and literary success are all, in a way, extraneous concerns. What matters is one's devotion to—and passion for—the work. For sentences. If you like sentences, you'll write for the thrill and challenge of it, dedicating yourself to honing your craft whether or not anyone is ever going to pay you for it or publish it.

Similarly, it might be good to stop and ask ourselves at this point whether or not we like people who are different from us, people who are mentally handicapped. Do we honestly answer, "No" or "Well . . ." That's fine. A no at this point does not have to be the end of the matter; we can grow to like—even grow to *love*—the mentally disabled. But we need to be open to that possibility—the strong likelihood that the mentally handicapped will become important to us. Because in the end there probably will never be enough time, resources, and staff to make special treatment of the mentally disabled possible in our churches. Yet outreach happens, and happens successfully. It is not the result of a big budget or specially trained instructors. It comes from the heartfelt work of people who believe the mentally handicapped are worth their time and effort. It comes from people who are learning to love the mentally disabled.

I don't believe most of our churches would turn their backs on a woman who could not read; they would search for a volunteer to teach her, so that she could discover the precious truths of Scripture for herself. We probably would think hard before informing a deaf man there was no room for him in our congregation; we would find (or train) someone to sign the songs and sermon for him. Rather than turning away from a child in a wheelchair, we would consider adding a ramp to our front walk. Rather than telling our shut-ins that we simply don't have time to visit them with Communion or a devotional, someone, somehow, would make the time.

Perhaps the difficulty for the church is that the illiterate and the physically handicapped can all recognize their desire for spiritual food—corporate worship, prayer, teaching, and fellowship—and speak up for themselves. Unless your congregation is blessed with especially committed advocates, there is no one to speak for the spiritual needs of the mentally handicapped. The mentally disabled will not write increasingly hostile notes on the back of registration cards; they probably won't tug on our sleeves and ask about getting involved in a Sunday school program; they won't make a scene when their spiritual needs go unmet. They will continue dutifully to attend, whether or not they are able to glean anything from their Sunday school class or the worship service. (At worst, they or their families will find a new church, one that does meet their needs.)

The Bible, though, encourages us to strive for more than mere reaction or response. It mentions loving one another and reaching out in love. So what is holding our churches back? In *Retarded Children: God's Children* Sigurd Petersen quoted a Kansas pastor who had come up with one theory.

> Why has the church shunted the retarded child out of its mind, heart, classrooms, and worship? Why the neglect shown these boys and girls? Is the church, after all, hard-hearted? Perhaps the reason why so few retarded children find a church home is because the church is *embarrassed* by them—embarrassed because it has not been taught how to meet the problems presented by retarded children.
>
> But the church has been "missing the boat." In its perennial search for dedicated stewards it has bypassed the child who is retarded—a child who has much to contribute to the life of any congregation. True, there are numerous problems presented by these boys and girls that the church does not face with "normal" children. But the retarded child can offer unique contributions.
>
> Properly guided, under illuminated leadership, these children *can* participate in the church's program of Christian education and worship—even though one seldom finds more than a few retarded children in a local church. Given tasks in proportion to their abilities, they can make themselves materially useful to the congregation's ongoing program. Seeing them, in

spite of their handicap, developing into useful and devoted servants gives a whole congregation new incentive. They offer us a challenge. Watching their minds open up in acceptance of God makes the entire church mindful of God's love even for these, His children.

Another Christian educator, Dorothy Clark, rhetorically wondered in *Teach Me, Please Teach Me,* "When Jesus commissioned his followers to go and make disciples of all mankind, did he intend to include the mentally retarded?" She adds,

> Many Christians feel the retarded cannot be reached for the Lord; that in fact they do not need to be. God, these church people say, has already provided for the salvation of the retarded since—in theological terms—they will never reach the age of accountability. . . .
>
> Christ promised not only eternal life, but abundant life as well. Therefore these who will forever remain as little children can and should receive the love, the joy, the peace, and the hope that only Our Lord provides. Yes, the mentally retarded need our Jesus for right now.

Why reach out if there is only a handful of mentally handicapped people in your community? Because every one of them is made in the image of God. Yes, there will be people we will never be able to reach with the gospel; their understanding might be limited to simply comprehending our attention and love. There even may be people who cannot notice even that; I believe that Martin, the profoundly mentally handicapped young man I visited with my father, was one. But even he could feel the warmth of our touch and hear the reassuring sound of human voices.

I am naive enough to believe that God can use even that for His glory.

Some might find it equally naive, or at least simplistic, to bring up at this point 1 Corinthians 13, often called the "love chapter." But if the Apostle Paul's words have no relevance for our interaction with the mentally handicapped, I wonder whether they can have any relevance at all. To my mind, they are the very foundation for human relationships.

> If I speak in the tongues of men and of angels, but have not love, I am only a resounding gong or a clanging cymbal. If I have the gift of prophecy and can fathom all mysteries and all knowledge, and if I have a faith that can move mountains, but have not love, I am nothing. If I give all I possess to the poor and surrender my body to the flames, but have not love, I gain nothing.
>
> Love is patient, love is kind. It does not envy, it does not boast, it is not proud. It is not rude, it is not self-seeking, it is not easily angered, it keeps no record of wrongs. Love does not delight in evil but rejoices with the truth. It always protects, always trusts, always hopes, always perseveres.
>
> Love never fails. But where there are prophecies, they will cease; where there are tongues, they will be stilled; where there is knowledge, it will pass away. For we know in part and we prophesy in part, but when perfection comes, the imperfect disappears. When I was a child, I talked like a child, I thought like a child, I reasoned like a child. When I became a man, I put childish ways behind me. Now we see but a poor reflection as in a mirror; then we shall see face to face. Now I know in part; then I shall know fully, even as I am fully known.

> And now these three remain: faith, hope and
> love. But the greatest of these is love.

Why should the church be involved in educating the mentally handicapped? Why should we be concerned for their spiritual lives? Why should we seek to develop friendships with them? There are three very simple reasons.

We are called to love. In addition to 1 Corinthians 13, we have John 13:34-35: "A new command I give you: Love one another. As I have loved you, so you must love one another. By this all men will know that you are my disciples, if you love one another." Loving, then, is the hallmark of being Christ's disciples. And love is a strange and wonderful thing for the mentally handicapped to receive. Often they face the stares and taunts of their normal peers; often they feel useless, wanting to contribute to society but rarely given the opportunity. A loving church provides a much-desired haven of security and opportunity. Many churchgoers speak of worship as a means of "recharging the batteries" so they can go back and face another week in the world. The church provides that same kind of refreshment for the mentally disabled, who may long for it more than the most beleaguered mother or harried executive among us.

We are called to disciple. The words "teach" and "train" appear over 100 times in the Bible, from God's command to Moses to "assemble the people before me to hear my words so that they may learn to revere me as long as they live in the land and may teach them to their children" (Deuteronomy 4:10) to this comprehensive passage in Titus 2:11-15:

> For the grace of God that brings salvation has appeared to all men. It teaches us to say "No" to ungodliness and worldly passions, and to live self-controlled, upright and godly lives in this present age,

> while we wait for the blessed hope—the glorious
> appearing of our great God and Savior, Jesus Christ,
> who gave himself for us to redeem us from all wicked-
> ness and to purify for himself a people that are his very
> own, eager to do what is good. These, then, are the
> things you should teach.

And, of course, many Christians claim as their motto
Matthew 28:19—"Go and make disciples of all nations"—
presented without amendment or qualification. Helping
others to learn more about God and grow in their appreciation of Him has always been a hallmark of fruitful
Christians. There is no reason to believe that the mentally
handicapped cannot share in the rewards of that fruitfulness.

We are called to deliver the message of salvation to the lost.
Again, in the Gospel of Mark Jesus tells His disciples, "Go
into all the world and preach the good news to all creation.
Whoever believes and is baptized will be saved" (Mark
16:15-16). Of course, we may encounter those who are
unable even to comprehend a simple message of God's love;
I believe they will be benefactors of God's infinite grace. But
to focus on those few is to ignore the majority of the mentally handicapped, people who *can* understand the basic
message of salvation and can respond. It is our responsibility to reach out to them as God's faithful witnesses.

THE POWER OF ACCEPTANCE

Recently my wife and I had the joy of buying our first house.
When we first began looking at properties with the help of
a realtor, I was overwhelmed by the disclosure form, the buy-
sell agreement, the buyer-broker form, and the inches of fine
print growing along the bottom margins like black weeds. It
was mind-numbing. I didn't realize that was only the begin-

ning; the paperwork only got worse when, one week later, we fell in love with a house and quickly applied for our first mortgage.

I came home from my second day at a brand-new job (in a brand-new industry) to a tableful of legal-size documents printed in triplicate. After dinner, as my wife, Sylvia, read aloud paragraph after paragraph of convoluted legalese—packed tight with terms that were nowhere defined—my brain clouded over. I kept asking her, "Who's the one who decided this can't be an easy, straightforward process? Why can't this be as simple as buying a car?"

When we last bought a car, we went to the dealer, told him what we could afford, were given a tour of the lot, picked a car, took a test drive, picked another, drove it, told him a little about our finances, wrote a check, signed two forms, and drove away. It took all of one morning.

That's what buying a house should be like. Or the same principle anyway; just with a lot more money at stake. Everyone involved seems to make it far more complicated than seems necessary.

That is also what I'd say if I could share a quiet cup of coffee with the survey respondent who wrote, "The issue of ministry to particular constituencies is just now emerging": "You're making this too difficult." "Ministry to particular constituencies" sounds an awful lot like committees, programs, plans. While there certainly is a place for those things as churches develop their ministries, I'm not so sure they're essential at the outset. In my opinion, if even one mentally handicapped person attends our church, we don't have an option about "ministering to that particular constituency": that particular "constituency" is sitting in our pew or our classroom, and he or she *wants to know God*. If that weren't the case, they wouldn't be there. Either we accept and work with the mentally disabled, or we ignore and thereby reject them. Our ministry begins with acceptance, with simply reaching out to the mentally handicapped as people.

Within the last ten years or so this approach to outreach has gained popularity as "friendship evangelism." While clear and descriptive, this phrase still sounds a bit like: "We'll become your friend because we want to convert you to Christianity; once we establish a relationship with you, the evangelist in us will leap out and set to work." It is a Trojan Horse approach that cheapens both the beauty of true friendship and the power of the gospel. Sharing the gospel as a result of sincere friendship is, I think, the most powerful form of witnessing. If our ministry to the mentally handicapped is to be effective, it will grow naturally as we reach out to them because we enjoy them as people, because we desire their friendship, and because they have much to share with us. If our only interest is in saving their souls or reaching their parents or covering all our demographic bases, I'd just as soon we didn't bother.

To be honest, this is an area that I think all of us struggle with from time to time. When I find myself falling into the trap—ironically, something that happens as I get further away from my childhood years, during which every older person was an authority figure—I can recall the example of my sister. Barbara desired friends with whom she could comfortably spend time, so she established friendships with many of her coworkers at the sheltered workshop where she is employed. She also made friends through church and, earlier in her life, through special-education classes at school. Inevitably her friends often became my friends too. Of course, I realized they were mentally handicapped; it made no difference then.

JoEllen lived at the youth home in town that cared for those under eighteen who may have been either mentally handicapped, orphaned, wards of the state, or between foster homes. JoEllen could best be described, perhaps, as "slow" rather than mentally handicapped. To me, she was just JoEllen, someone who came over on Saturday and Sunday afternoons to listen to music or play board games with Barbara and me.

For weeks I cherished the fact that JoEllen had taught me how to play Yahtzee, a game Barbara had received as a Christmas present one year. I joined the two of them often, thrilled to be playing such a grown-up game with my older sister and her friend. Then one day I had the misfortune of playing Yahtzee with some of my friends from school.

"What are you doing?" they asked as I tallied my score.

I explained.

"But that's not how you're supposed to play," they told me.

I stared at them, baffled.

"Haven't you ever read the rules?"

"Uh, no," I said. "A friend taught me."

"I don't know what your friend taught you," one said, "but it sure wasn't Yahtzee."

After their laughter subsided, I promised myself to double-check the rule books from then on.

Carol was another friend, and one whom Barbara still visits occasionally on weekends. I don't know how she and Barbara met. Carol helped out with her family's air conditioning/heating business and never worked at the sheltered workshop, and she didn't attend our church. Still, she and my sister shared a common circle of friends and a fondness for board games.

What they didn't share, thankfully, was a knack for imaginative storytelling that made every one of Carol's visits an adventure. We never knew what wild thing she was going to tell us next. One week she said that Norman, a mentally handicapped young man we all knew, had gotten married and went to Europe on his honeymoon. Just everyone had been at the wedding, she assured us. But the next week she just as emphatically told us that it hadn't been Norman, but a friend of his from the workshop. By the end of her Saturday visit, it was likely there hadn't been any wedding at all or that the marriage had already ended sadly in divorce.

I don't think Barbara took Carol's stories any more seriously than my parents or I. Still, those fanciful tales didn't shake Barbara's fondness for her friend. Make-believe happened to come along with the whole Carol package, just like bad driving skills or a fondness for gossip might be part of someone else's makeup; you might not appreciate those parts of his or her personality, but these stories don't erase the fact that a friend is still a *friend*. I can still see my mother rolling her eyes at me over Carol's latest story, but these stories were part of what gave Carol her unique personality.

Carol, JoEllen, Terry, Mary, Norman, Norma, and others enriched my childhood in ways I am only now beginning to appreciate. I thank God that I had the opportunity to know them all during a time before the prejudices of teen and adult life overtook my acceptance of them. Because of my experiences with them, I have a better understanding of the value of acceptance and its role as an important first step in outreach done in the name of God.

PUTTING FEET ON OUR FEELINGS

I realize, though, that something significant may have to happen before some congregations are willing or able to make that important first step. To be fair to the pastors and church leaders who responded to my survey, they may well be guarded in their optimism because of the resistance or reluctance they're feeling among their own nonhandicapped church members.

"Most people in the congregation suffer from a lack of understanding."

"The mentally disabled can be obnoxious to some."

"The normal children get into battles with them and withdraw because the others come to class or church."

"There's not much interest in doing anything special for the mentally handicapped."

"Folks seem to discount the mentally disabled person who attends."

"Some of their nonhandicapped peers have not been accepting."

"There is a lack of sensitivity to the need [to minister to the mentally disabled] on the part of some church members."

There *are* unique problems associated with reaching out to the mentally handicapped, even beyond the question of acceptance. (And I hope to deal with them honestly throughout the coming chapters.) Yet, despite the problems, there are remarkable successes that make the effort worthwhile.

One survey respondent told of a young woman who had previously visited church only under duress. Once there, she preferred to sit outside the classroom, in the hall, rather than join her class. She was unsmiling, unapproachable. But after a year of only a little effort on the part of the teacher and her helpers, the girl came to understand something of the accepting nature of God. She learned that, unlike some of the people she had met in her daily life, God cared deeply about her needs and about *her* as a person. God taught her those things through the loving outreach of her Sunday school class. As a result of this church's work, this student now attends services, smiles, and is much more friendly—mirroring her newfound faith and opening up to those around her rather than closing herself in.

Her teacher could easily have given up on her early on. After all, she is not equipped with a degree in psychology; she's not trained to work with the mentally handicapped. But she had the confidence to continue doing what she believed God wanted her to do. Acting on that—and out of the natural affection that had arisen for the woman—she was able to sidestep the initial nervousness and fear of the situation.

After all, every day each of us faces challenges that appear, at first glance, to be impossible, even insurmountable. Yet each day, if we are open to it, God's power strengthens us, enriches us, and enables us to accomplish what we could not have managed under our own steam. Joni Eareckson Tada and Gene Newman have written:

> A ministry to the disability community affords the church a wonderful opportunity to display God's magnificent, unconditional, and impartial love before the watching world. . . . I find it fascinating to see how God can take a ministry to the "unlovelies" and turn it into such a visible, concrete, and powerful display of his love. The apostle Paul, in his letter to the church at Corinth, expressed it well when he wrote, "But God chose the foolish things of the world to shame the wise; God chose the weak things of the world to shame the strong" (1 Cor. 1:27). . . .

> Discerning the opportunities behind the disguise
> is the challenge facing those who desire to establish
> disability ministry.

MEETING THE CHALLENGE

When teacher Dorothy Clark first considered developing a ministry to the mentally handicapped, she approached her first meeting, with twelve mentally disabled adults and children at a church workshop, with dread. It was "a day I literally prayed myself into," she wrote in her book *Look at Me, Please Look at Me*, a chronicle of her experiences. She explains:

> A concern for the spiritual needs of the handicapped had been growing within me. It became so persistent that I asked my secretary to pray with me for ways I might help in this needy area. Soon came the invitation to this workshop. "It's not safe to pray," my secretary said as she handed it to me, "unless you're ready for an answer."
>
> Now I was here, along with ten ministers from other churches and denominations—hesitant, awkward, and fearful of doing or saying the wrong thing.

Hesitant, awkward, fearful. Those are feelings all of us may have as we begin to work with the mentally handicapped and face the myriad of questions that hit us at the outset. Will we have the patience we'll need? Will we be able to present Bible truths simply enough for them to understand, but real enough to be understood as truth and not just another fairy tale? What teaching materials can we use that will work? Will we have to worry about discipline? Should we integrate the mentally disabled with their normal peers or establish special Sunday school classes? Would they learn best if placed in classes according to chronological age or mental age? And what about worship services? How can they serve God in ways that will benefit themselves as well as the rest of the congregation?

The questions are many, but so are the answers and the experiences of those people who have successfully established effective ministries to the mentally handicapped.

One such person is Rev. Roger Peters, a United Methodist minister and former head of the religion division of the American Association on Mental Retardation. A May 1994 Associated Press story told of his first experience with giving Communion to the severely mentally disabled. He had expected to feel absurd.

> What he discovered, instead, were unforgettable acts of faith in the faces of those who came before him.
>
> "In those moments, I experienced the clearest and deepest experience of the holy I have ever had in my life. The absurdity wasn't my communing persons with profound mental retardation. The absurdity was my thinking I could understand the mystery of God's presence reaching out to us." . . .
>
> The halting, broken language of a retarded individual simply inquiring "Holy communion?" before a service had convinced Peters long ago that a profound faith and mental retardation can go together.
>
> Without glorifying mental limitations, Peters said, he thinks retarded individuals can be seen as a spiritual treasure for showing people the possibility of "that kind of poignant experience of the holy . . . that touches us at the center of our being." . . .
>
> "Except you become simply who you are as a vulnerable human being, you cannot enter the kingdom of God," he said. "People with profound limitations don't have any pretenses, and they teach us something when they do that."

To become "simply who you are as a vulnerable human being" is the first step for anyone coming to Christ. Often it is only when we experience our vulnerability, our state of sheer neediness, that we see how utterly helpless we truly are when confronted with the weight of sin. Then, at last, we can set aside our own will to rest solely in the only One who *can* help us. And in so doing we discover the miracle of salvation. Simplicity and vulnerability are starting points for the mentally handicapped, but they are not worthy ends in themselves. The miracle of salvation awaits them as much as it does the rest of us.

In the following chapters we will look at specific teaching materials and approaches that will help give your ministry the best opportunity to reach out to the mentally disabled—and the best opportunity to absorb the lessons the mentally handicapped can teach us as well. The focus will be primarily on the Sunday school classroom, where intimate, even one-on-one, instruction—the kind of teaching that has the greatest impact on the mentally disabled—is most possible.

No one that I have heard from went into this kind of ministry full of assurance and free of questions. But be assured that as we spend time with the mentally handicapped, the hesitancy, awkwardness, and fear subside. They are replaced with the confident assurance that God is using us to meet the relational and spiritual needs of people who are very important to Him, having been made in His image and created for His purposes.

I believe that the lives of the mentally handicapped you touch will become an equally important part of your own life and the life of your church.

Chapter 4

TAKING THE
FIRST STEP

One person. In some churches, that's all it takes to set in motion a ministry to the mentally handicapped. It was that way at First Baptist Church in Defiance, Ohio, a church of about 350 members.

There was one parent in that congregation who felt that the spiritual needs of her mentally disabled daughter were going unmet by the standard Sunday school classes. Not that people weren't trying. But the classes, like nearly every other class in church or school, were almost entirely written-word based. That wasn't the way her daughter assimilated information. Words were too abstract; they required too much concentration. What her daughter needed instead was a class that would present biblical material visually and physically, with pictures and hands-on examples that would create tangible mental links with the information. So the mother talked with one of the pastors.

He listened to her concerns. He had never worked before with anyone who was mentally handicapped. But he had received some curriculum information that had been sent, unsolicited, in the mail. It looked as if it would fit this student's needs. Now all that was missing was a teacher.

"That's when my friend talked to me," said Sharon Baughman, the woman who is now First Baptist's teacher of handicapped adults. When her friend asked her to consider teaching a special class for the mentally disabled, Sharon's first reaction was apprehension. Yes, she had taught in the public schools, but she had no training or experience in working with the mentally handicapped. What would she say to the students? How could she know what to teach them? Would they listen? Could they understand? Would they recognize that the Bible stories, activities, and songs were not fairy tales but reflected something true and real that could change their lives?

Then she looked through the curriculum passed along by the pastor. It looked good, providing thorough explanations and step-by-step approaches. And it recommended an approach to teaching the mentally disabled that seemed to be the most effective. It was time for class.

That first Sunday, the class consisted of Sharon and her one student. But the student had mentally handicapped friends, and soon the class grew to two, then four, then five. The apprehension and fear Sharon had initially struggled with vanished as she worked side by side with her students and got to know them personally.

As of this writing, Sharon's class is one year old and five members strong. Students have learned much about God and His love and acceptance of them. They have also learned to reach out beyond their church's walls. Some students regularly visit shut-ins at a local nursing home, and the class recently chose to support a child in Africa; they take up regular offerings to provide the child with food and clothing.

Sharon does not manage this all on her own, however. Her particular curriculum recommends that one "teacher" is in charge of the opening and closing large-group sessions, while the actual lessons are to be taught by "mentors" who work one on one with students. She has five volunteers who serve as mentors, explaining any parts of the lesson that are proving difficult, talking about any personal issues the students raise, praying with the students. I couldn't help but remember how so many survey respondents had mentioned the lack of interest or support among their congregations, so I asked her how she was able to find enough volunteers to have a teacher-student ratio of 1:1. She seemed genuinely surprised by the question. She had never had any problems finding people to help.

Now, after a year of intentionally keeping the class size small, giving everyone the chance to acclimate themselves, the congregation is making a concerted effort to further advertise the class and help it to grow. What began with one student's special need and one mother's request has become an important part of the church's overall ministry.

Sharon Baughman's class is a textbook example of a successful Sunday school class for the mentally handicapped. Her students learn Bible truths, are discipled by caring helpers, and understand the gospel's message that faith leads to helping others—such as the elderly and the impoverished. The proof of the class's effectiveness is in its fruits.

The good news is that any congregation with a desire to help their mentally disabled visitors and members become Christians and grow in their faith can develop an active ministry. There is nothing special in the drinking water in Defiance, Ohio. And, trust me, Baptists don't have any secret, sacred knowledge when it comes to ministry. Sharon Baughman's church simply started with a need and took specific practical steps to meet that need. Any church can do the same.

The first step, explored in the previous chapter, is to determine the need and gauge the congregation's desire to act on that need. Step two is to understand the learning patterns of the mentally handicapped and settle on a teaching method and suitable resources that will most appeal to those patterns.

WHAT'S SO *SPECIAL* ABOUT EDUCATION?

As a high school student, I was vaguely aware that, operating alongside the classes I and all of my friends attended, there was one classroom that was set apart. I didn't know any of the students in it, didn't know what projects consumed their energies or what topics they discussed. About all I did know was the name—Special Education.

Special Education classes were held in a long, window-rich classroom across the hall from the auditorium where plays and assemblies were held. Regardless of a student's scholastic focus, practically everyone had to pass that room at least once during the day. I remember feeling both curious and embarrassed every time I walked by.

Looking back, that strikes me as odd. After all, I had spent every year of my life living with a mentally handicapped person. And for about two short years during her enrollment in the high school, Barbara had probably sat in that very classroom and looked out those same windows. If anyone should have known that nothing secretive or sinister happened there, it should have been me. Still, I couldn't stop myself from glancing in every time I went by.

Maybe the problem was that I simply didn't understand what they could do differently in that classroom that would actually *work*, that would help the mentally handicapped learn something. I assumed the students were taught the same things the rest of us were taught, just at a slower pace. Or maybe they focused more on basics like spelling and reading than on mathematics or social studies. I didn't really know what it was that made their education "special."

I have since learned that Special Education is "special" because it considers the limitations and general behavioral characteristics of the mentally handicapped and modifies teaching methods in order to lessen emphasis on the limitations and target the abilities. Despite my earlier theorizing, it is not a matter of teaching the same material at a slower pace. In Christian-education terms, it does not mean simply giving students Bible pictures to color or enunciating more clearly as we read the Scripture for the day. Truly reaching the mentally disabled student means understanding how she or he learns and using curriculum and/or teaching methods that reflect that understanding. And that will be true whether the mentally handicapped are in a class by themselves or are involved with a group of normal peers.

DIFFERENT NEEDS AND DIFFERENT APPROACHES

At her church in Ohio, Sharon Baughman's class is not advertised as being a class for the mentally handicapped. When announced in the bulletin or mentioned from the pulpit, it is described as a special class open to anyone who learns better through visual media rather than the written word. The words *mentally disabled* or *handicapped* are not used in relation to the class.

Sharon admits that such a description is confusing to some church members, who don't realize that the class is particularly suited to the abilities of the mentally handicapped. Even so, it has spoken clearly to their target audience, and the class is gaining interested students with almost no effort.

Drawing relationships between pictures/stories and life—as opposed to written words/stories and life—is only one specific learning characteristic of the mentally handicapped that requires a modified approach to teaching. The following ten learning traits of the mentally handicapped will also affect the kind of curriculum we choose and the way we present information in the classroom.

Generalities, abstractions, and big ideas have little meaning. The mentally disabled have difficulty seeing the relationship between generalities or abstractions and the way those big ideas directly relate to their own specific experience. For example, "God loves you" is an abstract idea with no real-word hooks for them to grab hold of. This trait is one reason why word-based learning is not the best way to reach the mentally disabled; words are abstractions, and it takes mental effort to see the connection between black shapes on a page and the ideas they represent.

For similar reasons, *applying a learned skill to another area or activity is difficult.* Just as they have problems seeing the relationships between general and specific ideas, the mentally handicapped have difficulty understanding how skills learned in one area can be used to accomplish a different kind of task.

Understanding in any form will come slowly. The mentally disabled are not equipped to grasp stories or ideas immediately. By the time their normal peers will be ready to move on, the mentally handicapped will just be warming up to their new subject.

Pictures, sounds, touch, smell, and taste are more eas-

ily understood than either spoken or written words. Any message that can be conveyed actively through the five senses will be much more quickly understood than those thoughts presented through more abstract means, such as reading or lecturing. The more the mentally disabled can personally interact with the message, the better. For example, the story of the woman who poured perfume on Jesus' feet could be augmented by bringing a bottle of real perfume to class for students to sniff.

Distractions are common. Unless the students are actively involved in the lesson—either through a hands-on activity or through close personal interaction—they will likely lose interest quickly, turning their attention to the window, to their neighbor, to entirely different topics.

Verbal communication skills are limited. I have mentioned that my sister does not care for questions. But that is not because she does not know how to answer; something often just closes down frequently when she finds herself under even the most innocuous scrutiny (such as, "What TV show are you watching?"). Barbara is not alone in this regard. Not only are question-and-answer and discussion-based classes out of the question, but teachers cannot expect much verbal feedback by which to gauge their effectiveness.

Motor skills are limited. While hands-on activities are certainly effective, the mentally handicapped often will not be able to participate in games that rely on physical skills or activities requiring good hand-eye coordination. It isn't only that certain skills are beyond their grasp; students will likely become frustrated when they see that the messages their brains are sending to their hands get twisted along the way and they cannot make themselves do what they want to do.

There may be little motivation to learn (*particularly at the beginning*). At the outset, students will not know what they are working toward, what the class has to offer. They may not be used to the whole idea of church, and so have no idea what to expect. Because of that, they may not see the point early on.

Attention spans are brief. As one curriculum for the mentally handicapped notes, it would not be unusual to not make it through an entire section of the lesson. Students can quickly lose interest and want to move on to something fresh.

Self-appreciation is low. The mentally disabled will likely come to our churches with at least some history of feeling out of place in the world. Peers and siblings—and sometimes even parents—have told them that they are dumb, stupid, ugly, unwanted. By the time they reach their teen years, mentally handicapped students might believe that.

Fortunately, these ten negatives can be met with corresponding, positive teaching techniques.

Speak simply, drawing lessons from the students' personal lives when possible. Make the lesson as relevant to each individual as possible.

Be patient in teaching the same idea or activity repeatedly as it arises throughout the course of a lesson.

Use simple instructions, simple words.

Speak simply and utilize, whenever possible, pictures, videos, songs, and hands-on object lessons that avoid the abstract.

Teach in small chunks, be willing to take breaks, and choose a classroom that will limit interruptions, visual and otherwise.

According to one curriculum, the three Rs for teaching the mentally handicapped are, *"repeat, repeat, repeat."*

Choose activities and/or games that do not require strong motor skills. Singing, for example, is a popular element in classes for the mentally handicapped.

Provide motivation by reinforcing correct answers as much as possible. Give them as many opportunities as you can to succeed in class.

Provide variety in the lesson; choose to involve students as much as possible rather than simply reading a lesson aloud to them. Be prepared to move on to the next point as soon as interest starts to wane.

When appropriate, be willing to touch your students and let them know you care about them. Assure them of God's love and concern for them. While they may not be able to conceptualize the phrase, "God loves you," they can certainly understand it when *you* love them. The understanding that you love them because God loves them can come later.

Of course, these points are by no means exhaustive. But they can help lead to ministry specially crafted for a mentally disabled audience, providing a foundation for building understanding and relationships. (An expanded list of resources that will aid in the understanding of and ministry to the mentally handicapped is included at the end of this book.)

CLASSROOM GOALS

As we are guided by the "big picture" goals of making disciples of all nations and loving others as much as we love ourselves, there are "small picture" goals that follow naturally from the above list of teaching tips and can help us specifically as we minister in a classroom setting. In a nutshell, these smaller goals answer the question, What can we really hope to accomplish for God and for the mentally handicapped as we develop a ministry for them?

The goals are simple ones:

Understand who God is and what He has done for the world.
Understand that God loves them and cares about them.
Learn significant Bible stories.
Learn to pray.
Respond to God's love in worship.
Accept Jesus as Savior.

In his book *77 Dynamic Ideas for the Christian Education of the Handicapped*, author James Pierson notes that "every lesson needs to have a specific goal that is leading to the accomplishment of a general goal. For example, if your general goal for a quarter is to develop a concept of God, the specific purpose for a lesson might be 'to learn that God made the birds.'" The lesson-specific goal, then, supports the broader goal of building awareness of God and His role in the world and in students' lives. Pierson goes on to say that achieving these specific goals is aided if several supporting factors are present.

An understanding of the student's neurological problem. This will help those teaching to recognize a student's natural limitations and idiosyncrasies. It may also help them to understand that activities that might otherwise be deemed "acting up" or willful are actually the result of a handicap totally outside the child's control.

Involved parents or guardians will encourage their children and charges at home, supporting and nurturing the work begun in the classroom.

A classroom that creates a positive learning environment. Limiting distractions will help. So will maintaining discipline, providing much verbal encouragement, and offering a caring touch. The goal is to create an environment in which students feel loved and are encouraged—by word and deed—to build community with one another.

A congregation that supports the ministry. Ministry to the mentally handicapped depends upon a willingness on the part of the congregation to open the church to people who may require extra patience and a larger number of volunteers than usual—and the rewards may be slow in coming.

MAINSTREAMING OR SPECIAL CLASSES?

The last few decades have seen increasing interest in "mainstreaming" students—that is, placing them among their nonhandicapped peers. In fact, I would guess that mainstreaming is considered by many to be, without question, the *right* way to reach the handicapped. The idea is that the mentally disabled will integrate more easily into society if they have not been closeted away from it for the duration of their education. In addition, it is believed that the examples of normal peers will stimulate them toward growth and development.

The decision of whether to mainstream or to develop special programs and classes is, of course, up to each individual church to make. But there are some important points to weigh as you consider that decision.

Mainstreaming may work best if you are teaching one or two mildly mentally handicapped students, or one or two students from a variety of age levels; special classes may be the answer if you find that you're regularly having four to six mentally handicapped students in the same age range. (One note: Among survey respondents who did mainstream their mentally disabled students, all but one placed handicapped students in the Sunday school class appropriate for their *age group*, rather than basing placement on *mental age/ability*.)

At nearly all of the churches I contacted, mentally handicapped students are integrated into regular classes.

That means they are taught the standard curriculum of their normal peers, at the same speed and with the same words and activities and examples. Personally, I believe that such an approach will benefit only the most mildly mentally disabled students, those who might simply be considered "slow" by the public schools. All others will find themselves having to learn like their nonhandicapped peers, and their unique learning needs will be ignored. In the end, their ability to understand who God is and what He can mean for their lives will be hampered.

My personal belief is that the mentally handicapped will learn best—and will develop the personal relationships with their teachers that lead to spiritual growth—in classes that are specifically devoted to their needs. Still, I realize that there is a price to pay for placing the mentally disabled in special classes. The mystery surrounding mental handicaps grows the fastest when the mentally handicapped are placed behind closed doors; once that occurs, fear and prejudice may follow. Yet, I think there are ways to effectively counter such fear and prejudice among church people—for example, through involving mentally disabled students in community service, encouraging them in activities that serve the whole church body, and allowing them to have visible involvement during worship services. In fact, public activities will go a long way toward building bridges of understanding and empathy within the Christian community.

And consider this: of those churches surveyed, every one that integrates students into normal classes rated the effectiveness of its mentally handicapped ministry as "nil," "very weak," "fair," or "5 on a scale of 10." There were only two exceptions. One was Calvin Christian Reformed Church in Sheboygan, Wisconsin, which rated its ministry "very effective." But the pastor, Rev. Steven Alsum, who has had a long and fruitful history of work with the mentally handicapped, went on to explain that his church tailors their programs to match their mentally disabled members' needs and that everyone pitches in to help lead their activities.

If your church is attended by very mildly mentally handicapped people who can thrive in normal classes, by all means try mainstreaming them. Or try mainstreaming if, like Rev. Alsum and Calvin Christian Reformed, your congregation has a strong commitment to meeting the needs of the mentally disabled and is willing to make an extra effort to do so. Otherwise, I believe your students and your congregation alike will benefit more from classes that address their unique needs with appropriate teaching methods and curriculum.

WHAT DO WE TEACH?

The question of what to teach, of what curriculum to use, will depend on whether or not your church decides to mainstream. If you do, your curriculum decisions have already been made; whatever curriculum is currently in use for normal classes will form the basis for teaching mentally handicapped students. But if you decide to establish special classes, curriculum help is available; you need not worry about having to write your own lessons or be frustrated trying to adapt a company's "standard" lessons to fit mentally disabled students' needs.

The first place to look for mentally handicapped-specific curriculum is within your own denomination. Several national denominations regularly produce materials for mentally disabled students, and using them would avoid concern about presenting viewpoints or information you might not endorse or feel comfortable with. For example, the Lutherans produce a wealth of material for the handicapped, but some Baptists would not care for the way baptism is presented. (On the other hand, most of the material for the mentally disabled will concern itself with the important biblical fundamentals that all orthodox Christians endorse and that mentally handicapped students can most easily grasp.) As you seek information, don't be afraid to order sample packets from the publishers. They may include student's and teacher's guides, as well as supplemental materials such as wall posters and craft/activity pages, and they will provide a good idea of how appropriate an entire curriculum line will be.

While it is good to begin with the products from your own denomination, don't stop there. You're looking for the curriculum that will meet your group's needs and will provide you with the resources necessary to teach effectively. Three companies' offerings are particularly worth evaluating, regardless of your denomination.

Concordia Publishing, a Lutheran publishing company in St. Louis, Missouri, offers "Our Life in Christ for Special Classes." This is a specially prepared teacher's guide that offers a quarter's worth of lessons. The guide leads the teacher from pre-session activities to opening worship, telling the Bible story for the week, using object lessons to help students apply the Bible to their lives, music and singing, closing, and post-lesson evaluation. In addition, each lesson opens with a list describing the central truth to pass along through the lesson, a memory verse, desired outcomes, and a list of additional materials needed (paper, markers, audiocassette, posters, etc.).

The material presented is clear and obviously the work of people who have experience teaching the mentally handicapped. If there is a drawback, it is that it assumes a certain level of Christian understanding that might not be present if students are more than moderately mentally disabled or if they are new to the church. For example, a lesson for December 5 told the teacher to set up a creche scene, gather students around, and ask, "What baby will use this manger for a bed at Christmas?" And next, "What's so important about the Baby Jesus?" Not only does this seem to be asking for more feedback than many mentally handicapped students will be able to provide, but it assumes prior knowledge of the Christmas events and an understanding of their significance. While memory verses encourage knowledge of the Bible, some teachers may decide that it takes so much time and repetition to help students recall the memory verses from week to week that laboring over them isn't worth the time it takes away from other activities, which are more hands-on and tangible and less reliant on students' mental abilities.

While the curriculum itself assumes some experience on the part of the teacher—and the class, for that matter—Concordia does offer a relatively inexpensive book entitled *How to Teach Special Students* that is very practical. It is a worthy purchase on its own.

Bethesda Lutheran Home Outreach Services, sponsored by Bethesda Lutheran Home in Watertown, Wisconsin, offers a broad range of resource materials and training resources, including workshops, pamphlets, teaching tools, videos, audiocassettes, bibliographies, and monographs. In this case, the curriculum comes in the form of a professionally produced newsletter—*Breakthrough*—that features highlights of denominational work with the mentally handicapped in addition to teaching material for a full quarter.

The curriculum section of *Breakthrough* includes lessons

with a particularly Lutheran perspective (for example, "Baptism" and "The Lord's Supper") as well as those with straightforward Bible-story themes, such as "The Parable of the Sower." It leads classes through opening songs (for the musical selections that are not reproduced in the newsletter, teachers are directed to the Lutheran hymnal), an introductory activity, guidelines for sharing the Bible story, and an activity.

Breakthrough will be most welcome in Lutheran congregations and by experienced teachers who have time for extensive background work. There is an incredible wealth of supplementary materials available through Bethesda; however, the actual curriculum can be vague. For instance, the entire instruction for an activity called "Role-Play Baptism" reads: "You can do a simple activity with a dish of water, a Bible and a baby doll. Or you can make it more involved with students taking the parts of parents, pastor and sponsors. In addition, consider going to the sanctuary to use the font." Nowhere is it stated what the teacher should *do* with the water, Bible, and doll. Also, drawing any real-life applications from the lessons is left solely to the teacher.

Although *Breakthrough* will have limited appeal to non-Lutherans, the resources offered by Bethesda are definitely worth serious consideration. They are invaluable for any church that is considering or involved in ministry to the mentally handicapped.

Friendship Ministries, a division of the Christian Reformed Church located in Grand Rapids, Michigan, emphasizes a one-to-one approach to teaching that enables classes to adapt lessons to individual needs and builds friendships between students and others in the church. That means every student has the attention of his or her own teacher.

Typically classes using Friendship materials begin with a short social time followed by group singing, prayer, and a Bible story. Next the group splits up among its teachers, who reinforce the Bible lesson through conversation and related activities. This lasts fifteen to twenty minutes and is followed by a closing social time with refreshments, which includes the entire group as well as any family members who want to attend.

The curriculum itself follows a three-year schedule that focuses on God (year 1), Jesus (year 2), and the Holy Spirit (year 3) through Bible stories and contemporary examples. It includes a group leader's guide, a teacher's guide, and student resources that include take-home papers with a simple retelling of the Bible story, illustrations, and related activities. The teacher's guide, the primary teaching tool for the lesson, features a simple lesson truth, lesson aims, background information for the Scripture, tips for presenting the material to students, and a list of required supplementary materials (appropriate activity sheets, a pencil, glue). Curriculum comes in "Youth" (ages ten to twenty) and "Adult" versions. Although developed by the Christian Reformed denomination, Friendship curriculum is used by denominations ranging from various Baptist groups to the Salvation Army.

For smaller churches, where building social ties is not something that has to be worked at, Friendship may be overkill. But for mid-to-large churches, it provides an excellent means for reaching the mentally handicapped with the *whole truth* of the gospel; it presents the gospel, and it also builds relationships and encourages outreach on the students' part. Given the one-to-one nature of the teaching, though, it requires a strong commitment of volunteer support from the entire congregation.

GETTING GOING

When Sharon Baughman's class for the mentally handi-capped began, the church made the decision to start small, and to do no advertising or canvassing for students for the first year, so teachers and students and church members alike could get used to the arrangement as quickly and easily as possible. Your congregation may wish to take a similar approach. But once that first year is behind you, or if a class built around one or two students begins to falter due to lack of attendance, it may be time to consider a specific push for additional students.

RECRUITING STUDENTS

Even though your church may be located in a small, rural town, you might be surprised at the number of mentally handicapped people in the population. It is a cliché that we miss seeing things in life if we aren't specifically looking for them; that is no less true where the mentally disabled are concerned. You may be convinced only one or two students are interested in your program—until the word gets out and families you knew nothing about eagerly approach you for more information.

To get the word out, first place a regular announcement in the church bulletin or newsletter. A standing announce-ment that appears every week will have the most impact. Otherwise, insert a mention of the class at least once a month, and as often as possible when visitors are most likely (Christmas, Easter, Mother's Day). If your church has a reg-ular column on the "church page" in the community news-paper, consider running a mention of the class there—or better, writing an article.

Next, prepare a flyer that can be distributed to special-education classes in public schools, agencies serving the mentally handicapped, area nursing homes and group homes that might have mentally disabled residents, and sheltered workshops. Post the flyer on the announcement board at the local grocery store.

Invite families of current students to provide the names and phone numbers of students' friends who don't currently attend, and enlist a class volunteer to follow-up with a personal invitation. Offer to arrange transportation for those students whose families cannot bring them.

BUILDING CONGREGATIONAL SUPPORT

If starting a special class for the mentally handicapped was at first clouded with problems or doubts from the congregation, you will want to brag about the people who have since gotten involved; as church members see and hear of others' participation in the class, they will begin to rally around the need for it. At the same time, if the church was 100 percent behind the program from the start, they will appreciate the assurance that comes from knowing their decision was a sound one.

A number of churches invite mentally handicapped members to serve as greeters, collect the offering, sing in the choir, and help with the youth group. This might require a bit of crusading on the part of the teachers involved, but the rewards will be worth the effort as people see how the spiritual lives of the mentally disabled are being affected by the church's ministry.

Another way to bridge the gap between the mentally handicapped and the rest of the congregation is through allowing them to play a part in the worship service, perhaps through solos, drama, or a simple Bible reading.

At my former church in Illinois, five minutes every Sunday was devoted to a "Ministry Moment," a time when a representative from one of the church's ongoing ministries would stand at the podium and give their personal testimony about what that ministry has meant to them. One Sunday it was about the church's small-group program. The next, a woman spoke about the church's support group for victims of sexual abuse. The following week, two nursery workers spoke about their pleasure in caring for all the babies in the church. All to let the members know what their church was accomplishing, and to let visitors know what opportunities were available. If your church has room for a similar presentation, a teacher and student might stand together at the front as the teacher describes the mission of the class.

GROWING COMMUNITY

Over the last two years our previous church has shifted its worship style from a traditional one (marked by hymns, the doxology, and choir anthems) to a more contemporary one (with choruses, "Ministry Moments," upbeat soloists) in an effort to appeal more to the modern church visitor. The strategy has worked; attendance has increased, ministries have flourished, visitors have become believers. The problem was, as much as I enjoyed the contemporary approach, sometimes I really longed for something with a little more age to it, a worship style that smells warm and musty, like an old church library. Some of my wife's and my friends desired that too. The difference is, they left the church to find it. Sylvia and I stayed (until new jobs in Michigan pulled us away). The reason for us was community.

Simply put, we really loved the people we went to church with. We had shared hard moments with them; we had cried, eaten, laughed, sung, and prayed together. Much as I longed for an echo of the liturgy I had once enjoyed as an Episcopalian, I would not—could not—abandon those church relationships just because I sometimes hankered to hear the Lord's Prayer.

Community is the real-life living out of biblical truth. It will develop naturally among church members as they grow in their understanding and love of the mentally disabled they are helping to reach. It's practically a given among the mentally handicapped themselves. But as your class grows in their own understanding of God's Word, a new desire for community might arise, a desire for outreach. If so, consider that a giant step has been made in their acceptance of the Bible's message. And be willing to act on it, because that will have a profound affect on your students' lives.

Acting on this might involve taking the class to visit a local nursing home once a month so they can spend time visiting with the residents. Or it might involve a Saturday spent picking up the litter at a local park. Or, like Sharon Baughman's class, it might mean reaching out all the way to Africa, to help a child who needs food, clothing, and other necessities.

The mentally handicapped are hands-on people. As your students grow in their understanding of the Bible's message, they will want to take their knowledge of God's love and act on it, using their abilities to improve the lives of those around them. Those who give will be blessed. Those who receive will be blessed. And those who never expected the mentally disabled to be able to give at all will turn red with joyful embarrassment.

Chapter 5

THE BENEFITS OF
OUTREACH

After working for eleven years in the marketing and editorial departments of several Christian book publishers, I decided to shift careers and focus more on writing than editing. That change took me and my wife from the Chicago suburbs, where we'd lived since college, back to her hometown of Charlotte, near Lansing, Michigan. Now writing is not only my avocation, it is my full-time job—creating press releases, public relations materials, articles, speeches, and advertisements. To move successfully from editing to ad writing, I had to shift from focussing on a product's *features* to clarifying the *benefits*. And I think something similar happens as churches make the shift from having minimal or unplanned outreach to building a ministry for the mentally handicapped.

In advertising, successful copywriters are adept at taking the facts about a product and translating them into results that fulfill the customer's needs or desires. For example, to announce that a church has both contemporary and traditional Sunday morning worship services is to highlight a *feature* of the church, a plain fact that doesn't draw any connection between that fact and the potential churchgoer. But to explain that the church has come up with this arrangement "so that every member's unique spiritual needs might be met" is to introduce a benefit. Likewise, a church member might brag to church-wary friends that the pastor's sermons never last more than fifteen minutes. That's a feature, and it might earn a yawn or a "So what?" But if that same church member can say, "Because Pastor Dave's sermons never last more than fifteen minutes, we always have enough time to get home, get dinner on the table by noon, and catch the start of the game," that will be perceived as a benefit. Don't get me wrong—I'm not saying that we should push benefits in such a way that we compromise on the proclamation of truth. But it is possible to be too light on the benefits angle too. Let me explain.

I wonder if too many churches that *want* to minister to the mentally handicapped get hung up on the "features" of their program (or proposed program) and overlook the benefits. Before they've encountered a single mentally disabled person, committees might get lost in discussions about whether or not to mainstream their students. Average churchgoers who feel that they should be doing something for the mentally handicapped can fritter away their energy fretting over how to have a conversation with the mentally handicapped. Christian educators can get caught up in discussions of class size, curriculum, volunteers, classroom availability. In the process, we can lose sight of the benefits—which likely will be shared on both sides of the relationship.

For the many pastors who expressed their frustration openly—"We'd love to do something for the mentally disabled, but we don't know how to reach them"—my goal in this chapter is to encourage them to not lose sight of the benefits of Christian outreach. We can easily feel over-whelmed by the "right" and "wrong" ways to convey the gospel to the mentally handicapped, the myriad teaching tools and resources that are available, the varying abilities of students, the availability of interested teachers, and on and on. But if we let those concerns stop us before we even get started—or cripple a ministry that is still in its early stages—we've gotten hung up on the *process* and missed the *promise* of fruitful ministry to the mentally handicapped.

THE GIFTS WE GIVE

The promise is twofold: first, that the mentally handicapped will come to accept and experience God's love for them; and, second, that we who minister to the mentally disabled will find our own faith deepened.

What aspects of Christianity can we realistically hope to pass along to the mentally handicapped? Scripture offers some helpful goals. Psalm 19:7-8 notes that "the law of the Lord is perfect, reviving the soul. The statutes of the Lord are trust-worthy, making wise the simple. The precepts of the Lord are right, giving joy to the heart. The commands of the Lord are radiant, giving light to the eyes." Later, the Psalmist wrote:

> Your statutes are wonderful; therefore I obey them. The unfolding of your words gives light; it gives understanding to the simple. I open my mouth and pant, longing for your commands. Turn to me and have mercy on me, as you always do to those who love your name. Direct my footsteps according to your word; let no sin rule over me. Redeem me from the oppression of men, that I may obey your precepts. Make your face shine upon your servant and teach me your decrees. (Psalm 119:129-135)

Both of these passages speak of the simple receiving wisdom and understanding through the Word of God. But they each mention numerous other benefits as well, benefits that certainly are viable possibilities in the spiritual lives of the mentally handicapped, those who might be today's "simple" people.

Pulling from these passages just the phrases and concepts that speak of results yields this list: reviving the soul, making wise the simple, giving joy to the heart, giving light to the eyes, obedience, understanding, longing, love of God, steadfastness, and education. Will we successfully pass along every single one of these? Maybe, but not likely. Still, these are excellent goals nonetheless—and they are basic enough to be *reasonable* goals for the majority of mildly and moderately handicapped individuals whom we will serve. In addition, they will be the natural result when Sunday school classes specifically tailored to the needs of the mentally disabled (along the lines discussed in the previous chapter) are combined with the exemplary lifestyles provided by teachers, volunteers, and others in the church.

By reaching out to the mentally handicapped, churches also can instill a basic sense of self-worth and accomplishment. As we remind them again and again through our actions and words that they are truly important to us and to God, we give them a gift that few—if any—others in their lives are offering.

Sigurd Petersen described the fruits of faith among some of the mentally handicapped children who had come to live in the group home he oversaw:

> Laura is a severely handicapped girl of sixteen. . . .
> From all indications she has had good religious training. She has experienced acceptance in her church

and a good relationship with her Sunday school teacher. She talks about her Christian faith, her Baptism, and her participation in the Lord's Supper. She has her own prayer life and says that prayer relieves her feelings of stress. She can remember my sermons and has the ability to accept their message with feeling. . . .

June has spent most of her thirteen years in an institution, the last five with us. She is a pleasant, outgoing, moderately retarded girl. Recently she said: "I have learned about God and Jesus and not to cuss. I pray to Jesus for forgiveness, for Jesus forgives. Doesn't he?" . . .

One of the most touching incidents that has come to my attention was reported by James's teacher. James is an undersized seven-year-old. He has an enlarged and deformed head, with only one eye. His teacher had given him a picture of Jesus with a little child on his lap. James, with his one eye, looked at the picture and said: "That boy has a big head. Jesus loves him. He loves me too."

There is one more important gift we can give: trust. This comes in the form of responsibility, the value of which was noted by all the churches I contacted that considered their ministries to be effective. That could mean that we trust our mentally handicapped churchgoers to sing in the choir, take the offering, greet people at the front door, usher, serve food at the Wednesday-night dinner, work in the nursery, mow the lawn, or stuff envelopes for church mailings.

The opportunities are great. At one church, an eighteen-year-old girl with Down syndrome has learned to do sign language and now interprets for the deaf during Sunday services. Elsewhere, a mentally handicapped boy plays the trombone with his church's brass section. At another church, a group of mentally disabled members participates in the annual "living Nativity" in December. To some of us who are not mentally handicapped, these might be small things. Maybe they would even be the kind of minor church obligations we would try to get out of if asked. To the mentally disabled, they mean acceptance. And for those who live constantly with the reminder that they are not like other people, acceptance is a wonderful gift.

THE GIFTS THEY GIVE

Anyone who has spent time working with the mentally handicapped can attest that they have received just as much as they gave. The return is not necessarily seen in increased intellectual prowess or manual achievement; after a year some students may still not know the words to a song sung every Sunday. But the benefits for those who share a church building, a pew, or a classroom with the mentally disabled are real just the same. They help us to glimpse parts of God's personality we might otherwise miss—the delight in beauty, the value of a warm embrace, the constant surprise of the world around us. The mentally handicapped help us to see ourselves, our world, and our God with fresh eyes.

Any contact at all with the mentally disabled is likely to leave us with a lasting memory. For example, I carry with me a relatively unimportant memory that has lingered for many years, of Donald, a tall, mentally handicapped man in his mid-twenties, stepping through the doors of my home church on a Sunday morning long ago. At that time he was a new Christian, and he wore his faith like a medal. I remember that a brilliant smile beamed from his face, and he clutched a jet-black Bible tightly under his arm, as if he feared losing it. I cannot say what the gospel meant to Donald intellectually, but I can report without a doubt how he felt about it in his heart: he *glowed*. I was too young and too uncertain of my own faith to have had any personal impact on Donald's Christianity. Instead, he impacted *my* Christianity, giving me an example of what a joyful and new faith looks like. It was beaming from his face. I turn to that face even now, twenty years later. Whenever it seems the gospel message is in danger of getting lost in a maze of Jesus theories, New Age influences, "post-Christian" rhetoric, and plain old theological claptrap, I summon up the memory of Donald coming to church. Because of his example, I immediately recall the flush of excitement I once felt myself after discovering the meaning of God's Word for my life.

Writer Gloria Hawley glimpsed something special of God's grace after she gave birth to two mentally handicapped children. At first she wrestled with God's plan for her life, as well as His plan for her children, wondering perhaps what reward could ever come from having two children who were handicapped. In time, though, she realized that God's Word could speak as much to the mentally disabled as to the normal, so she began reading Scripture aloud to her son and daughter. Their reactions were mixed: "Craig became helpless with laughter, while Laura smiled politely and put fingers in her ears." It was apparent to her that Craig and Laura needed the Scripture to be related specifically to their own lives before it would hold any meaning for them. They weren't able to make the connections on their own.

She began by "personalizing" Psalm 23 for her daughter, substituting the name "Laura" at the appropriate points and providing simplified imagery that Laura would understand. The experiment worked; Laura was "delighted and animated" by her mother's paraphrase. Soon Laura's teacher and her speech therapist were calling to find out what Gloria was doing at home to make the girl so responsive and bubbly. When Gloria explained that she was reading Scripture aloud, Laura's speech therapist said, "Well, if it works, do it. Send the Scripture along, and we'll work on it here too." For Gloria, Laura's progress was a miracle of awakening.

The miracle repeated itself with her son, Craig. As Christmas approached, Gloria read and reread for him the story of the first Christmas from the book of Luke. Soon there was another phone call, this time from Craig's special-education teacher.

> Craig's teacher called and, in tears, described how [Craig] had told his class about Jesus' birth—the star, God's love, angels and shepherds.
>
> Our little boy, his eyes shining with the light that split the heavens so long ago, spilled over with God's message of unchanging love—to a group of abnormal children no one had thought to tell before.
>
> Craig's ministry had begun.

Gloria closed her story by noting that "Craig and Laura remain handicapped. God has not chosen to 'heal' them. He is pleased to use them."

That is a sentiment shared by teacher Jane Dahl in *Look at Me, Please Look at Me*. Her story of an important lesson she learned from a group of handicapped children is worth relating in its entirety.

> I was seated near the back of the room watching Dorothy [another teacher] interact with the class. Carrying a mixed bouquet, she walked down the aisle encouraging different ones to touch and smell the blossoms. Taking the hand of a blind boy, she guided it over the petals of a rose. Then brushing his fingers

along the stem, she explained, "Those sharp things are thorns, Hal."

Turning her attention to the class, she asked, "Because there are things about this flower that aren't so beautiful, should we throw it away?"

"No" was the popular reply.

Then arranging the bouquet in a vase, she likened people to the flowers—all different, yet each one beautiful in its own way. Selecting a daisy, she looked around the room. "I might have something wrong with me—like this flower might have something wrong with it." As Dorothy spoke, she pulled a petal from the daisy. "Perhaps you have a problem, too," a second then third petal fell to the table, "like an arm or leg that doesn't work. Or maybe you can't read, or it's hard for you to talk. But God loves us just as we are." By now five or six petals lay scattered on the table.

Across the aisle from me six-year-old Susie sat teetering in her chair. When Dorothy began plucking at the flower, Susie's eyes widened and her mouth dropped downward. Suddenly, she scurried up the aisle.

The room was still as the tiny figure gathered up the petals one by one. Cupping them in her hands, she offered Dorothy the bits of flower.

As Dorothy reached to receive the offering, Susie summarized the lesson in one brief statement, "It's all right—Jesus will fix it!"

As she bounced back to her seat, I surveyed the room. There were many things that needed fixing—twisted bodies, mute tongues, deaf ears, blind eyes, and retarded minds. Each child represented a depth of heartache inconceivable to families with normal children.

I thought of my own little niece. "Hey, Jane," my brother-in-law shouted over the phone, "It's a girl!"

Three months later the diagnosis came—permanent brain damage.

How easy to turn from God in such tragedy—to question the reconcilability of a compassionate God with malformed babies. Yet, God does not turn from the handicapped. He is more concerned for them than the fallen sparrow; He numbers the hairs of their heads, also. Yes, God loves them, every one.

How do I know this? Susie told me . . . and David . . . and Molly . . . and Ruth . . . and Jim . . . and Millie . . . and Paula . . . and Doreen . . .

The mentally handicapped are not unfinished people waiting to be made complete before they can bring glory to God. Neither must they conform to anyone else's idea of what they ought to be before God can use them. They are "right" just as they are.

I am reminded of a passage from Fannie Flagg's nostalgic, heartbreaking novel *Fried Green Tomatoes at the Whistle Stop Cafe*, in which Mrs. Threadgoode, an elderly resident of the Rose Terrace Nursing Home in Alabama, tells a visitor how her husband, Cleo, had told her the doctors' diagnosis concerning their son, Albert.

> "He went on to tell me that the doctors up to the clinic said, although Albert may very well be physically sound and live a long and healthy life, that most likely he will never develop mentally past the age of four or five years. That he would remain a child all his life. And sometimes the burden of having a child like that, one that required constant attention, was too great. Cleo said that there are special places that . . . I stopped him right in midsentence. 'Burden!' I said. 'How could that precious, sweet baby ever be a burden?' How could anybody ever think such a thing? Why, from the minute he was born, Albert was the joy

of my life. There wasn't a purer soul that ever lived on this earth. And years later, whenever I would get to feeling a little down, I would just look at Albert. I had to work every day of my life to be good, and it was just a natural thing with him. He never had an unkind thought. Didn't even know the meaning of the word *evil*.

"A lot of people might have been sad to have a birth-injured child, but I think the good Lord made him like that so he wouldn't have to suffer. He never even knew there were mean people on this earth. He just loved everybody and everybody loved him. I truly believe in my heart that he was an angel that God sent down to me, and sometimes I cain't wait to get to heaven to see him again. He was my pal, and I miss him. . . ."

Graciously, God responds to the mentally handicapped just as He responds to all of us who are imperfect, sinful: He loves them and uses them just as they are, blemishes and all. As He brings about His will in their lives, our lives cannot help but be touched as well.

OUTSIDE, LOOKING IN

Ironically, the church may be more open to seeing God's hand at work in the mentally handicapped than their own families are. Inside the family, too often other emotions cloud people's perceptions. As you develop a ministry to the mentally disabled, chances are that other family members will be drawn in as well. The following points should be kept in mind as your church seeks to understand their needs and concerns.

Parents of the mentally handicapped—whether Christians or not—may carry with them feelings of regret, jealousy, guilt, and anger that blind them to the true potential of their mentally disabled son, daughter, brother, or sister. From the moment when a family physician or a public school teacher first suggests the possibility that something is wrong with a child, these feelings doggedly haunt every significant age in the child's life—from when he *should* be learning the alphabet to when "everyone else" her age is married and raising a family. Families experience regret that their child's handicap will keep her or him from enjoying the full scope of life; jealousy toward the majority of families whose children are not born mentally disabled; guilt because, deep down, they probably harbor feelings of responsibility for their child's condition (regardless of whether or not such feelings have any logical support); and anger at God for giving them the burden of a handicapped child.

Although I have never wrestled with guilt in relation to my sister, I certainly have experienced a range of negative emotions that have made it more difficult than it should have been to appreciate every facet of a sister like Barbara. What helped me the most was seeing how others—particularly those who supervise her at the sheltered workshop where she is employed—enjoyed her company and understood her. Their reaction helped convince me that I had been missing something.

Just as a prophet must leave his hometown to find people who will respect him, so the mentally handicapped can often find a sympathetic reception from those outside the family who are able to see them solely for what they are, with eyes unclouded by regret, jealousy, guilt, and anger. Many mentally disabled people are finding such receptive people in Christian churches today, among congregations who have made a place in their programs and their hearts for the mentally handicapped.

THE GREATEST BENEFIT

Ministry is at its best when it opens a two-way street between those who are serving and those who are being served. Perhaps that's the real point of outreach: to help others even as the relationships we establish mold us into better people.

The idea applies just as well to work with the mentally handicapped. Hopefully, we will share the truths of Scripture, teach about prayer and faith, share stories of God's goodness and love—and our listeners will understand and respond. But at the same time we will be learning of God's love and grace, of the importance of simplicity, of God's power to change lives regardless of their IQs. That shared learning, that reciprocal growth, is one of the greatest benefits of ministering to the mentally disabled. It's what we can honestly tell those who might ask, "What's in it for me?" It's what we have every right to work and pray for.

Joan Dubberke tells the story of a young mentally handicapped woman named Karma and how her simple testimony affected an entire congregation.

The church first met Karma when she came to Sunday school; she was twenty-one years old and absolutely silent—either unable or unwilling to speak a word. As time went on, however, Karma grew accustomed to the other students and her surroundings. She began to feel a part of the class, and she began to learn that the lessons were meant for her as much as anyone else. Although she never spoke, she learned to convey her understanding to her teacher with a smile; a frown meant that she needed help.

Over the years it seemed that Karma grew in her understanding of God and His love for her, and she indicated that she wanted to be baptized, like her Christian mother.

Karma's father, however, was not a Christian, and he did not approve. Finally, after fourteen years of attending church, Karma received her father's consent to be baptized.

When the pastor visited her Sunday school class in preparation for the ritual, he asked her, "Do you believe you are a sinner?" Karma nodded her head. "Are you sorry for your sins?" Again, she gave him a vigorous nod. "Who took your sins away?" the pastor asked.

With that, Karma rose to her feet, went to the altar at the front of the classroom, and picked up the cross standing there. She wrapped her arms around it and hugged it tightly to her chest. That simple, silent, and eloquent act of devotion left no doubt of her sincerity. It was a moment that Karma's Sunday school class never forgot, a shared grace that transformed Karma's life even as it left its mark on untold others.

One last example along these lines:

A pastor in Southern Carolina told me that years ago a baby who was diagnosed as hydrocephalic was born in the congregation. Because the child had "almost no brain," her doctors gave her little chance for any sort of meaningful existence. In the crudest terms, she would be nothing but a vegetable. With medicine providing no answers, the church rallied around the family and pledged themselves to pray for them. Then a miracle happened. The little girl's brain began to develop. Eventually the doctors were forced to revise their prognosis from "vegetable" to "she'll never be more than a C student"! That experience of answered prayer, of seeing God's hand at work in the life of a mentally handicapped person in their midst, rallied that church as few things could. To this day, years after the family has moved away, that girl has left her mark on her church family.

THE HANDICAPPED-FRIENDLY CHURCH

In her book *Alzheimer's: Caring for Your Loved One, Caring for Yourself*, author Sharon Fish shares a story that many families of the mentally handicapped can relate to as well. The daughter of a mother with Alzheimer's, she yearned to find a church that would understand both her mother's needs and her own.

. One Sunday she visited a church that had established a reputation of reaching out to Alzheimer's sufferers. When she arrived, she saw that there was ample handicapped parking and a ramp for wheelchairs. Inside, space was allocated for wheelchairs in the aisles. So far, so good. But the church showed its true colors during the sermon.

A church member named Hoppy suffered from dementia, and every Sunday it so happened that the pastor would say one thing or another that would trigger in Hoppy's mind some familiar song.

The Sunday that Sharon visited, the pastor was preaching about heaven. And when he happened to say that heaven would be every believer's eternal *home*, Hoppy suddenly stood up and began to loudly sing "Home on the Range." Sharon held her breath, wondering how the congregation would react. She could just imagine the eyes of every person in the sanctuary focusing on the man and his family.

She couldn't have imagined what happened next. As Hoppy continued to sing, the pastor smiled and motioned for the congregation to stand with him. Then they all joined with Hoppy to sing a rousing chorus of "Home on the Range." When they had finished, everyone sat down, and the pastor went on with his sermon.

This, Sharon realized, *is a church that understands!*

Every family of the mentally handicapped would rejoice at such an understanding and unflappable group of people. But such congregations don't just come together by chance. They occur when folks have had the chance to get to know one another, to share a conversation or a cup of coffee between services or a ride to Sunday school or a common interest in television shows or fast food. In this case, unlike the adage, familiarity breeds understanding, not contempt. And understanding will help all of us—whether family or friends of the mentally handicapped—to remove whatever blinders we may be encumbered with and to see the mentally disabled through God's eyes.

The people at Christ's Wesleyan Church in Egg Harbor, New Jersey, have made a commitment to creating such a welcoming environment. There sixteen mentally handicapped people (four are church members) regularly attend worship services and participate in Sunday school, as well as other ministries. How do they do it? The pastor has a straightforward response. "We don't allow it to be an option for including the mentally handicapped in all activities," he told me. If there are normal members of the congregation who don't care for the arrangement, "we suggest they find another church. Our 'under-developed' people stay. This is non-negotiable with us!"

If your church is just beginning to consider ministry to the mentally handicapped, you might be tempted to disregard a church like Christ's Wesleyan, saying, "Sixteen mentally handicapped people—no wonder they have a successful ministry. I don't think there are sixteen mentally handicapped persons in our whole town!" That may be true. But don't bet on it. You may be amazed at the number of individuals who will seek your program out once they hear of it.

After all, there are five to seven million mentally handicapped people in the United States alone; 100,000 to 200,000 are born every year. The majority are not locked away in institutions but are living in open communities, with family or on their own. As your church establishes a reputation for itself as a welcoming place for the mentally disabled, they will find you. Like *Field of Dreams'* mythic baseball diamond in the middle of an Iowa cornfield, if we build a mentally handicapped-friendly church—even if we do so in small-town Iowa—those who need it will come.

Think of it happening in slow stages. Maybe right now you have no mentally handicapped members or visitors. Or maybe you have only one or two. And you can hear yourself or your leaders making comments like these pastors and teachers:

"One mentally handicapped individual is a member of our church. But we minister to a small village; I don't know of anyone else in the community who might come" (Flanagan, Illinois).

"One person attends and is a member, but we are just a small church" (Harbor Beach, Michigan).

"Families have attended with handicapped children from time to time, but they have left because of no effective ministries for their particular needs" (Arlington, Washington).

"We are open to making a deliberate effort to reach the mentally and physically handicapped. One mentally handicapped young man is a member, and he is special and precious to us" (Raleigh, North Carolina).

"The only mentally handicapped person attends worship services, as our theology emphasizes worship. Beyond that, there is nothing for the girl" (Brooklyn Center, Minnesota).

"There is a group home for the mentally handicapped in the neighborhood; individuals are ministered to as they are here, but there is no outreach program" (Bakersfield, California).

"Four mentally handicapped people attend, and two are church members" (Decatur, Georgia).

"Only one young lady comes occasionally with friends" (Alexandria, Michigan).

"We took one mentally handicapped person into membership and made friends with another, but neither are involved in Sunday school" (Wellston, Ohio).

"Two attend, but neither are members" (Lebanon, Virginia).

"Three attend, but none are members. We do love them" (Delhi, California).

"Both mentally handicapped members live in group homes. They are both active and dearly loved by the members and are included in all phases of church planning, insofar as they are able to participate" (Pittsboro, North Carolina).

"Both mentally handicapped individuals are under fifteen years and are official church members. Some people 'plan' ministry; others just do it. We just do it" (Sheboygan, Wisconsin).

Although the majority of the churches I surveyed told me their outreach was practically nonexistent, many expressed a desire to move beyond the initial stages and really make a difference in the lives of the mentally handicapped. Frankly, it doesn't take an awful lot more than that simple desire to shift outreach to a higher level.

As our churches see the mentally disabled come to know and accept the message of the Bible, they will realize that word-of-mouth advertising is just as effective in the mentally handicapped community as it is elsewhere. The people who find joy and love and acceptance among our congregations will tell their friends, their families, their coworkers. As Gloria Hawley's son, Craig, made plain, it is very hard for the mentally disabled to remain quiet about the things that excite them. Donald's shining face was like a beacon drawing others. The mentally handicapped *will* tell others, and those others will want to know firsthand what all the excitement is about. If you have one mentally handicapped person attending services, your outreach is ready to take off.

How can I be so sure? I grew up in the small town of Centralia, Illinois, a fairly typical rural community of 14,000 to 16,000 people. No one would expect it to be a hotbed of activity where the mentally handicapped are concerned. But not long after my family moved there in the late sixties, my father recognized the need for a place where mentally disabled people like my sister could spend time constructively, perhaps even performing jobs that would benefit others as well as themselves. He made contact with several other parents of the mentally handicapped who felt the same way.

In 1967 Kaskaskia Workshop, Centralia's first sheltered workshop for the mentally disabled, was chartered. In 1969 the workshop hired its first two paid staff people to oversee the contract work of seven mentally handicapped workers.

When I visited the workshop in 1978, there were just over seventy mentally handicapped workers. By the mid-1980s that number had tripled. Today there is a staff of fifty-six and more than 275 mentally handicapped individuals who come to work five days a week. Are all the employees from Centralia? No. Some live in the nearby towns of Sandoval, Salem, Odin, Nashville, and numerous points in between. But the workshop offers something for each of them that makes the long ride worthwhile. Once word got out about the workshop, the mentally disabled and their parents chose to go out of their way to take advantage of it.

I believe the same thing can happen with any church that discovers the benefits of reaching out to the mentally handicapped.

THEY ARE ONLY PEOPLE

In an earlier chapter, I noted the disservice we do the mentally handicapped when we look at them and see only guileless, simple innocence. While this chapter has focused on the good fruits that flourish in the rich soil of a dynamic ministry, it would not be fair to simply leave it at that. After all, much as the fictional Mrs. Threadgoode may like to believe it of her dear son, Albert, the mentally disabled are not flesh-and-blood angels; they are people, with the same mix of pleasant and unpleasant traits we all carry around with us. The same applies to the church, where Christians are not always angelic in their attitudes and behavior.

Choosing to have a ministry to the mentally handicapped will bring out the best and the worst in all concerned. But that doesn't mean your ministry must suffer as a result. Equipped with the knowledge of what to expect and how to cope with difficult situations will help your congregation work its way constructively toward solutions that will answer the needs and concerns of everyone involved. That is the focus of Chapter 6.

Chapter 6

THE CHALLENGES OF OUTREACH

"Empathy. 1. Identification with and understanding of another's situation, feelings, and motives."

THE AMERICAN HERITAGE DICTIONARY

Where there is charity and wisdom, there is neither fear nor ignorance. Where there is patience and humility, there is neither anger nor vexation. . . . Where there is peace and meditation, there is neither anxiety nor doubt.

THE COUNSELS OF THE HOLY FATHER SAINT FRANCIS,
ADMONITION 27

Train a child in the way he should go, and when he is old he will not turn from it.

PROVERBS 22:6

There are challenges in reaching out to the mentally handicapped that are more fundamental than the decision whether or not to mainstream or where to locate a workable curriculum. They arise from the fact that the mentally disabled are human beings just like us, people who just happen to have had their learning processes slowed down. Why should that cause challenges? Because it's easy to miss seeing them just as people, with everyday concerns, interests, and needs. It is easy to see them as *so* different that we forget our many shared common interests and experiences, or to assume that one mentally handicapped person is probably just like the next and so can be reached with identical methods.

Even the way we often refer to them as "simple" people can cause us to stumble in our outreach. On the one hand the word fits: they understand simple concepts and simple words. But as human beings they are anything but simple. They are complex people—just like us—whose responses and thought processes cannot be predicted. When we deal exclusively with normal people, we generally know how to get our ideas across, how to communicate clearly, how to gauge one another's attitudes and needs. When working with the mentally handicapped, there will be remnants of that kind of relationship, but communication and interaction won't be nearly so cut and dried. And therein lie the challenges as well as the joys of effective outreach.

It would be easy for me to speak enthusiastically of the joys and let the challenges go unnoticed. But that wouldn't be fair to the mentally disabled or to those wanting to minister to them. And it probably wouldn't jibe with your own experiences if you're planning or already involved with a ministry to the mentally disabled; chances are, you've already fielded questions, concerns, and objections from church members. You may have even raised some of your own. But while I am devoting this chapter to a discussion of the challenges—and I do prefer that positive word to its more negative-sounding cousin *problems*—I hope that, by placing it after the chapter on the joys of outreach, you will similarly place the challenges in their proper perspective.

There will be growing pains with the start of any new ministry. And there will be concerns on the part of church members that are unique to a ministry to the mentally handicapped. Those who sit beside the mentally disabled in church will have their own questions, as will the normal students who share a Sunday school classroom with the mentally handicapped. This chapter will explore solutions to the most common challenges. And keep in mind that, like the physical act of childbirth, the pains of spiritual "birthing" give way to pleasure as both "parents" and "children" experience the fruits of the labor.

Scene 1: The news surprised the congregation at First and Foremost Faith Church: a group home for the mentally handicapped was scheduled to open in six months in the abandoned house next to the church building. Later, two months before the opening date, church members discussed the situation at the twice-annual business meeting.

"To be honest," the pastor said, rising to his feet, "I think this is a great opportunity for our church. We can take the lead in our community when it comes to reaching out to these handicapped people. They will be away from families, hungry for some friendly faces and acceptance. And I think we can offer that to them."

"But won't it be dangerous living next to them?" The questioner had taught Sunday school in the church for thirty-two years.

"Dangerous?"

"Well, I haven't had much contact with those folks myself, but aren't they temperamental—kind of unpredictable physically, I mean?"

A second church member spoke up. "I read about a woman who was mentally ill, Pastor. Much as I appreciate what you're trying to do, I don't think we can do much for them. It was sad about this woman in the book—here she had raised a whole family and all, but she ended up nailing an ordinary napkin to the living room wall like a painting because she thought she could see a man's face in it."

A third added, "If it's anything like Alzheimer's, we can't really expect them to get any better. They just get worse and worse until they die."

"Pastor, you know none of us is trained to work with special people."

"What if they want to sing in the choir?"

"I wouldn't even know the first thing to say to one of them."

"We've already had to combine the Young Marrieds with the Parents of Newborns class. I don't know where you're hoping to put a special class for the mentally disabled."

"And to be honest, some of us have our hands full with the *normal* junior highers, let alone adding handicapped students to the mix."

The pastor took a deep breath and glanced at his board of elders. They were watching him with a mixture of "We sympathize, Pastor" and "We told you so." Beside him, the church secretary was already scratching the discussion of the group home from the agenda. But, undaunted, the pastor vowed that within a week he would have a response for every objection and comment raised. He knew outreach to the mentally handicapped was important; he just didn't know yet how to convey that to his congregation.

Scene 2: Sunday morning in the senior-high Sunday-school classroom at First and Foremost, two months after the group home opened. This morning there were seven students in class; two of them were mentally handicapped.

"Karen," the teacher said, "can you tell the class about Jesus' talk with the woman at the well?"

"I love Jesus," Karen answered, smiling broadly.

"We all do, honey. But do you know what Jesus said to the woman at the well?"

Scott, a boy in the corner who was tilting his chair on its back legs, raised his hand. "Mrs. Jeffers, I know what they talked about."

"I imagine you do, Scott, but I'm asking Karen."

"You're always asking Karen. Or Chris," Scott muttered.

Mrs. Jeffers frowned. "Do you have something to say?"

"No." Scott took a breath. "It's just that this used to be an OK class. We read the Bible and discussed things and prayed and all, but it wasn't like we were following some lesson set in stone. I mean, we talked about faith and what it meant for us today, in the real world."

"And something has changed?"

"Definitely," Vicki added from the front row. She turned to Karen and Chris, who were sitting beside each other behind her. "You know how much we like having you guys in our class—"

"Speak for yourself," someone interrupted.

"—but, you know," Karen went on, "you . . . well . . . you learn . . ."

"Karen and Scott learn differently than the rest of you," Mrs. Jeffers finished, nodding.

"Right. The same thing—over and over and over again," someone said from the back row.

"We know it's important that they understand the lesson," Vicki added, "but I guess the rest of us just aren't getting much out of it anymore."

"Maybe we could have a class of our own," Chris said. "Some of my friends said they would like that."

"Mine too," Karen added.

Mrs. Jeffers shook her head. "We'd love to do that for you both—for you *and* your friends—but we just don't have the extra space or the extra helpers to make it happen. For now, I'm afraid we're all in this class together."

Scott let the front legs of his chair hit the floor with a thud. "Then I think you're going to see some of us heading for the church down the block."

FROM THE CONGREGATION

Unless a ministry to the mentally handicapped has been long established, or unless a new ministry to them has been building slowly and subtly over time, chances are good that there will be questions among the congregation about the decision to specifically target the mentally disabled.

For example, most normal people do not have a clear understanding of what mental retardation is and isn't. Because of their ignorance, they are apt to believe many of the rumors and myths that have circulated about the mentally handicapped for decades, fables that endow the mentally disabled with odd proclivities or sinister motives for their every action.

They also may equate mental handicaps with mental illness or "craziness." While the mentally handicapped *can* display the symptoms of mental illness, the two are by no means synonymous. As explored in Chapter 2, mental handicaps are the result of physical or chemical damage that leads to a slowing down or loss of mental functions—in short, brain damage that cannot be repaired. Mental illness, however, is chemically and psychologically rooted; it can often be treated with drugs and counseling. Those who bear the burden of mental illness (a susceptibility to which can sometimes be passed from generation to generation) may evidence it through erratic sleep patterns, extreme mood swings, and inexplicable behavior.

My sister, it seems, is mentally ill in addition to having suffered brain damage very early in her life. There have been times in her life when she lived utterly in her own world, locked away from the voice of reason offered by her family and from the constantly changing medications a succession of doctors have prescribed. For instance, there were months when Barbara read every scrap of information in the house about cancer, absolutely convinced that her body was full of it. After using the toilet, she would turn and stare into the bowl, hoping to have expelled the cancer at last, and watch as it swirled away from her. There were years when she did little but stare at photographs of the male leader of a gospel music group that my father had helped start. For at least several weeks, Barbara was obsessed with the story of the Lindbergh kidnapping, buying a book on the topic that seemed beyond her reading level, muttering fragments of the story under her breath at the dinner table. What was the catalyst for such fixations? Why did they involve her so completely? And what caused them to fade eventually, until they became even less than a memory? Apart from the effectiveness of several psychological drugs and the caring concern of trained doctors and therapists, I have no idea.

I would guess that Barbara's behavior during these low points was frustrating for her Sunday school teachers. During such times she tends to withdraw completely and be even more quiet than usual in groups. If the teachers expected any involvement from her, they would be sorely disappointed. It may be similar if there are mentally handicapped students in your church who also must deal with mental illness. They also might evidence behavior that is nothing like Barbara's. That is the challenge of reaching them.

However, it is only that—a challenge. While it would

not be fair to an unsuspecting congregation to let them assume that every mentally handicapped person in the world is emotionally healthy and psychologically predictable, it is also unfair to let them think they are opening a Pandora's Box of problems when they open their doors to the mentally disabled. Just as the mentally handicapped can be aided by careful, attentive instruction and love, so also those who also suffer from mental illness can be aided by medication, counseling, and a large dose of patience. Church workers might even be able to improve the latter's treatment, as they can offer feedback to parents or guardians about a student's actions while in their class; they might well witness behavior that no one else has been aware of.

(As I wrote the above description of my sister, I found myself wondering if any of Barbara's friends may also be mentally ill and how that situation might manifest itself. For a moment I had concluded that, yes, probably Barbara's friend Carol suffered some form of mental illness; after all, she used to tell such wild stories about everyone she knew. But I stopped myself at that point. Not only do I have no professional training whatsoever in mental illness or psychology that would equip me to make such a judgment, but I had forgotten how important fantasies and fairy tales are in the lives of children, who create stories of make-believe at the drop of a "Once upon a time." And the mentally handicapped can be very much like children. Rather than attribute Carol's fantasies to any form of illness, I think it is far more likely that she is simply enjoying the childlike pleasure of creating. I'd encourage others who, like me, are not qualified to make medical diagnoses to avoid embarrassment by sharing their opinions only with their favorite pet.)

Church members may also subconsciously wrestle with the social stigma that has surrounded the mentally handicapped for much of their history. After all, none of us enjoyed being called "stupid" or "dummy" or "retard" when we were in school. It's no surprise that, in order to disassociate ourselves from such insults and prove them groundless, we would do everything we could to show others we were nothing like the "slower" kids—we were *normal*. No matter how long ago we might have heard them, those playground taunts stick with us. (Depending upon the audience, you can almost always see a wisecrack just behind a listener's smile when you first announce, "We want to start a class for the mentally handicapped." Chances are, they have a relative in mind whom they'd love to recommend.)

Lack of volunteers is a third stumbling block to effective ministry. Without committed volunteers who will pledge to teach it, no curriculum, no matter how expertly written or devised, will get one foot off the ground. Without volunteers to drive the church van or offer rides, many students from neighboring communities won't be able to attend. Unless your church is large enough to support a paid position for ministry to the mentally handicapped—and I have yet to hear of one—the success of your program will depend on those who give of their time and personal resources to make it work. Many churches responded to my survey by saying they had no one who would shoulder responsibility for outreach to the mentally handicapped.

FINDING SOLUTIONS

Though significant and worthy of discussion, these difficulties need not thwart us from doing what we believe God wants us to do.

To offset the rumors and misunderstandings that many people still hold about the mentally handicapped, make books and articles about the mentally disabled available through your church library. (A list of sources used in this book is included at the end; an annotated bibliography of additional resources follows it.) You might also consider running small excerpts from such publications in the Sunday bulletin.

Allow the mentally handicapped to be seen by the congregation as much as possible. The greater exposure the average churchgoer has to her or his mentally disabled peers, the more they will be challenged to understand and accept them. You may want to feature your ministry to the mentally handicapped on a "Disability Awareness" Sunday, when special announcements about the church's program for the handicapped are made from the pulpit; you could even host a light social following morning worship and invite the congregation to meet the students. (Students who are able could be responsible for baking cookies or making other refreshments.) As the congregation sees the mentally disabled increasingly involved in activities that are productive and worshipful—whether by being in the choir, the church orchestra, or a drama group, or helping out by serving at a potluck, collecting the offering, greeting at the front door, and so on—stereotypical preconceptions and misperceptions will be replaced with flesh-and-blood *individuals*, people as unique in their personalities as the pastoral staff.

Lastly, the most important audience to win over is the pastor and other pastoral staff. The pastor's response to outreach to the mentally handicapped will set the tone for the entire congregation. If your pastor is fully supportive, you should have little problem finding volunteers, classroom space, and the budget for special curriculum and supplies.

FROM NORMAL STUDENTS

If it is not possible to create a special class exclusively for the mentally handicapped, Sunday school teachers will face the problems that arise as a result of mainstreaming. In addition to those problems experienced by the general congregation, normal students—and I'm speaking primarily of children and teenagers in this section—who sit beside their mentally disabled classmates will have concerns all their own.

Of course, that should not really surprise us. Consider the teaching approach that works best with the mentally handicapped: repetition, repetition, repetition; many breaks; willingness to quickly change subjects or emphases; small, simple, everyday stories; easily accomplished activities. Normal students—especially older high schoolers who may be psychologically and emotionally prepared to understand how the Bible applies to such "big ideas" as environmental concerns, abortion, contemporary ethics, sexual temptations, etc.—may well wonder what needs of their own can be met in a class that meets the needs of the mentally disabled.

In addition, some sensitive students may be afraid of doing or saying the wrong thing, fearful of an unexpected reaction or of thwarting any good resulting from the class. They will not be comfortable interacting with the mentally handicapped and may withdraw into their own groups rather than risk saying something stupid or being drawn further into conversation.

Others will be battling the social stigma that still accompanies mental handicaps. Churchgoing may already be a habit that junior highers and high schoolers try to keep secret; adding the presence of someone they feel socially compelled to shun might be too much for them.

Lastly, every normal student may at times have feelings of jealousy and resentment as a teacher constantly reinforces even the smallest sign of progress among mentally handicapped students. Teachers may also be inclined to touch their mentally handicapped students more and to simply devote more time to their concerns; after all, they may reason, such students *need* a teacher's help more than the normal students do.

That is undoubtedly true. But unless steps are taken to meet the needs of *both* kinds of students early on, chances are that there will be few normal students left to worry about after a few months.

One step that will help build unity among class members is making the commitment to spend the opening portion of each class period sharing prayer requests and personal needs that God and others in the class could assist with. As students learn more about the way their classmates spend their weeks—and what worries and difficulties they face in life—they will begin to appreciate one another. As students pledge to pray for each other, they will create a bond in Christ that could not exist by any other means. If this approach does not work for a specific class, try spending the end of each period in a social time, inviting the families of both mentally handicapped and normal students. Although this could potentially result in a classroom divided into clearly distinct groups, teachers will have an advantage in scheduling such social times for the end of class; if they can think of nothing else to talk about, students could discuss the lesson and any prayer requests or answers to prayer that may have been mentioned earlier.

Once the foundation for understanding and empathy has been laid down, other problems that arise will be easier to deal with. Students may be more willing to make allowances for slower learners once they've had a chance to know them. And as they witness their mentally handicapped peers' progress, they may even take steps to help out—encouraging, touching, tutoring, and explaining. As a result, they may grow spiritually in ways that could not have happened had there simply been Sunday school "as usual."

Still, teachers cannot afford to neglect the very real spiritual needs of their normal students. As much as possible, encourage mentally handicapped and normal students to interact, sharing ideas, examples from their own lives, and favorite activities. And be willing to approach normal students with the idea that their role in this class is not that of a sponge—attending class solely to see what can be soaked up effortlessly and taken away—but of a minister. Realistically, they may not end up discovering everything they wanted to know about a biblical approach to euthanasia or the differences between *agape*, *phileo*, and *eros*. What they will discover, however, is the personality of Christ. Like the congregation at large, they will take away from their experience with the mentally handicapped just as much— if not more—than they gave.

FROM THE HANDICAPPED

Normal students are not the only ones who have adjustments to make as they learn and work alongside people who are different than they are. Handicapped students themselves will also wrestle with a variety of emotions, personal experiences and histories, and abilities as they share classrooms with normal peers. However, awareness of these hurdles is the first step toward minimizing their effects.

Although most mildly or moderately mentally handicapped students will probably understand casual references to popular television shows or know the name of the President, there is a universe of information they may lack completely. For example, some may have spent their lives in foster families or sheltered homes and have little or no exposure to traditional family situations or loving, accepting relationships with normal people who are willing to sit and talk with them for the pleasure of their company (and who aren't either a doctor, nurse, or social worker). Discussions or stories that rely on so-called common knowledge may leave these students in the dust. Along similar lines, while some students may be mainstreamed in the public schools just as they are at church, others—who may not have participated in a public or private school that includes normal students—may be unable to relate to examples or discussions that focus on class experiences, homework, specific teachers, etc.

It is likely that every mentally handicapped student in class will represent a different stage of mental and emotional growth; depending upon the particular students, it may be unrealistic to expect the three mentally handicapped eighteen-year-olds to be as homogeneous in their thought processes, experiences, and behavior as three normal eighteen-year-olds in the same class. Each one is struggling against a unique level of handicapping brain damage. Each one may need a slightly different spin on the information they're presented so that it makes sense to *them*.

Before leaving the more mental/emotional concerns, it is worth remembering that the mentally handicapped are not blind to their condition. They certainly will recognize when their normal classmates answer questions more easily, don't receive as much attention, and get bored. Small feelings of jealousy may arise as they consider how they *should* be acting, what they *should* be able to know. But these feelings may also lead to a lowering of their self-esteem unless efforts are made to continually keep them mindful of their worth in your eyes and in God's.

Earlier chapters have already noted the short attention span and easy distractibility of the mentally disabled. Impatience, a harsh tone, or even discipline will do no good; these behaviors are outside mentally handicapped students' control. Teachers must simply be patient and be willing to move their lesson along as much as possible to keep up with the students, or perhaps stay ahead. Even normal students may appreciate and learn better at a pace more in keeping with the speed of their entertainment or emotional involvement.

There are other behaviors that will require teachers' patience. Some mentally handicapped individuals experience uncontrollable vocalizing. This could be something as simple as speaking out of turn, which might be corrected by explaining that in class everybody is to let someone finish what he or she is saying before they speak up. Others, though, may make random noises or have developed verbal "tics," such as singing or humming at inopportune times. Like those in the paragraph above, these behaviors may be unintentional and outside the student's control. If a teacher suspects otherwise, there is nothing wrong with her asking the student to behave in a more appropriate manner. If a statement such as, "I would appreciate it, John, if you didn't sing right now—why don't you sing me that song when class is over?" does not yield the intended result, or if the behavior is repeated in other situations, it is best to assume that it is involuntary and should be tolerated. Once that assumption is made, it will help the class to move on if the teacher could explain to everyone in the class—not just the mentally handicapped students—that "for John, singing may be as uncontrollable as blinking and it shouldn't affect how we feel about him." In a situation like this, the class might even choose to take a short break to listen to John's song. Chances are that the Christian acceptance John would experience would be just as valuable to him as the lesson itself.

Some mentally handicapped students may experience a range of additional physical handicaps as well. Some may need to remain in wheelchairs; others may be hard of hearing, unable to communicate verbally, not have the use of their hands, or struggle with incontinence. As much as possible, the church must be willing to make concessions for these students. If, for example, there is no wheelchair access to the second floor of the education building, either move classes to an accessible floor or make certain there are strong helpers to lift the chair and its occupant up and down the steps. In addition, teachers should allow for frequent bathroom and water-fountain breaks. If all but a few students are able to participate in an activity, an alternate and equally instructive and entertaining activity should be offered to those few, so that all in the class are treated fairly.

Lastly, I need to note that at least two pastors I contacted for this book mentioned the difficulties they've experienced with mentally handicapped attenders who also are battling alcoholism. Admittedly, that is less than 3 percent of the respondents; it does not seem to reflect a widespread problem. (In fact, during my research I read of only a few other such instances.) Still, if even one mentally handicapped student is also an alcoholic, your challenge to reach her or him will be great. Because the mental handicaps will remain a constant, I would recommend working first to help the student experience healing of the addiction to alcohol. If your church sponsors Alcoholics Anonymous meetings or some type of Christian-based support group, invite your student to accompany you, and be willing to help him or her to understand what is happening. Make an extra effort not to preach against alcohol but to instead emphasize your appreciation for the student, letting him know that God values him highly. As his self-respect grows, he may discover he no longer needs the support of alcohol. In the end, there can be no easy solution, no quick fix. While the effects of alcohol addiction may not manifest themselves in the course of Sunday school or worship services, they will certainly stand in the way of a student's growth mentally and emotionally, as well as spiritually.

If our primary purpose for outreach is to change those whose lives we touch with God's grace, we owe it to our students to involve ourselves in their lives as true friends, not just teachers, ministers, social workers, or volunteers.

THE PLACE OF DISCIPLINE

I do not personally believe that discipline will be a big problem among churches reaching out to the mentally handicapped. I have witnessed almost nothing that I would describe as intentional misbehavior on their part. In fact, the opposite is more generally true: the mentally handicapped want to please others more than anything else.

Still, when problems arise, it may be helpful to keep in mind a general rule of thumb: teachers or supervisors should probably not be comfortable allowing mentally handicapped students to do anything that they would not allow a normal six-year-old to do. That includes talking out of turn or interrupting others or disrupting the class with inappropriate sounds or actions (assuming these behaviors are within the student's control). What are the appropriate responses when such behaviors manifest themselves? That may depend on a leader's personality.

> It all began during the craft time one afternoon. I was passing out materials when Joe, one of the teenage boys, decided to try out for the Bolshoi Ballet. Had it been one of the smaller boys, I would have picked him up and set him in a chair. Joe's six-foot frame prevented that, however.
>
> So, instead, I rushed across the room and planted myself in the path of the stomping, yelling youth. "If you don't stop this racket at once," I warned, "I'm going to wup you!" . . .
>
> Like a balloon expelling air in frantic flight, Joe whirled to a gradual stop. "What," he asked, "is 'wup'?"
>
> His puzzled expression caught me off guard. In the momentary calm that followed, Joe grabbed my arm. "Now, now, Dorothy," he cooed soothingly, "take it easy. Everything is going to be all right."
>
> I had used those same words time and again to comfort an unhappy, frustrated child. Now Joe was using them to comfort me instead!

The narrator of this story, Dorothy Clark, goes on to note that the mentally handicapped, like their normal counterparts, feel more secure and valued when reasonable boundaries for behavior have been established. Boundaries, or rules, let the mentally disabled know that they are responsible for their behavior and that someone else trusts them to behave responsibly. As a result, they are willing to establish relationships of trust and responsiveness with the person who has established the limits. "When discipline has been established and is a familiar part of the child's training," Clark writes, "the resultant benefits will not be limited to the child alone.

The . . . teacher's attitude will brighten when he knows he has control due to the child's prior disciplinary training."

But what constitutes an acceptable level of discipline? I believe it's safe to assume that Ms. Clark wasn't really going to "wup" anybody. Yet she does say that if Joe had been smaller, she would have picked him up and set him in a chair. Are you willing to do that? Are others? For some church workers, physical contact like that might border on corporal punishment, something they would be very uncomfortable with. For others, however, picking a student up and setting him in a chair is a small action, and one that will benefit the class—whose time is being taken up by the more rowdy student—and the misbehaving student himself— who may get a surprising and valuable lesson in just how far he can bend the rules before they break. Touch has a powerful effect on the mentally handicapped.

Ultimately, how discipline will be carried out needs to be decided by each individual church, ideally in cooperation with the parents or guardians of the mentally handicapped students. But why not involve the mentally disabled themselves in such a discussion as well, asking them what they feel the best response to a situation would be based on their own experiences? If all parties can agree to procedures beforehand, everyone in the classroom will know what's expected and what will happen if they behave inappropriately. And the church can get on with the business of being the church, avoiding, as much as possible, the role of disciplinarian.

WE CANNOT DO IT—BUT MAYBE *I* CAN

Lastly, I want to address the possibility that despite your best efforts or those of your leaders your church has failed in its outreach to the mentally handicapped. Maybe you are a parent who has waged an uphill battle to get the church to do something constructive for your mentally disabled child. Maybe you are a social worker who, encouraged by the progress made in sheltered workshops, has tried and tried to get your church to develop similar programs, only to feel that you were talking to a federal bureaucracy. Maybe you are a pastor who could not get your congregation to share your vision for ministry. Maybe you are a lone teacher for the mentally handicapped who simply got burned out. Regardless of the circumstance, the result is the same: despite desire and effort, your congregation has not been able to serve the needs of the mentally disabled.

If that is the case, you have my sympathies and my understanding. I have seen churches with successful ministries, and I have seen those where ministries just never got off the ground. No one needs to be blamed for that. But I would encourage you to ask yourself one question: do I still feel called to minister to the mentally handicapped?

You see, I'm assuming that you felt a supernatural tug at the start; otherwise you would never have set out on such an ambitious project. But do you still feel that pull on your heart and mind? Do you still long to reach out to the mentally handicapped?

If the honest answer is no, that's fine. Certainly not all Christians are called to this kind of ministry. You owe it to yourself and your Lord to discover your real passions and pursue them for His glory. But if the honest answer is yes— even a quiet, hesitant, anxious yes—I would encourage you to follow your heart and God's call.

This book is ostensibly about how the church can meet the spiritual needs of the mentally handicapped. But what is the church? The church is its people, the body of believers. And if, in terms of ministering to the mentally disabled, that body of believers is all of one member strong, then so be it. Take up your call and act.

If you personally know a mentally handicapped individual, suggest meeting with him or her one-on-one for devotions or start your own small Bible study group for the mentally disabled in your home. Visit a local nursing home or group home where there are mentally handicapped residents and meet with them, offering to pray with them, read Scripture, sing songs, and discuss their spiritual concerns. Invite them to accompany you to church. Do you play the guitar? If so, take it along with you and lead group singing. In short, do whatever you need to do to establish and build friendships with those you wish to serve.

I pray that God will richly bless your efforts.

Chapter 7

A PERSONAL PERSPECTIVE

The concern of the church for its handicapped people of all types should be a continuous activity within its normal program. It should not be a light that flickers for a moment and then dies. It must become an educated dedication to a task of infinite significance to the spiritual life of the church.

SIGURD PETERSEN,
RETARDED CHILDREN: GOD'S CHILDREN

In the mid-1970s an obscure Christian advertising campaign swept the country, appearing on everything from buttons and bumper stickers to billboards and television. "I Found It!" shouted white letters against a blue-sky background (if my memory serves), as if they were written on the heavens. As if they should mean something to the average person.

The "I Found It!" campaign was meant to spark controversy, generate interest, and pique curiosity. All so that when squadrons of would-be evangelists appeared on your doorstep to "take a survey," you'd be intrigued by their "I Found It!" lapel buttons and the hint that, if the survey were endured, the secret of what that elusive "It!" was would be revealed at last.

I was a member of one of those squadrons. After a brief training session we had driven several towns over to collect our paraphernalia (buttons, clipboards, "surveys"), receive long lists of typed addresses (in those pre-personal computer days), and spill out of our vans, trickling down every street in town to spread the Good News. That's what the "It!" turned out to be: the gospel of Jesus Christ.

So what did this "survey" have to do with it?

The "survey" was our foot in the door. It was a masterfully written piece of propaganda that enabled us to establish conversations with strangers ("making cold calls," in sales jargon) who were willing to answer what we termed "research questions." But part of the way through the questions, the survey shifted its focus away from personal likes and dislikes, concentrating on spiritual needs and the interviewee's questions about God and faith. The belief was that the survey was so well crafted that it could lead the interviewee straight to God. And we had been instructed in the proper replies and comments, the evangelistic responses that would walk them step by step toward a commitment of faith.

At the time, though I was a nervous high schooler who had never really witnessed much, I thought it seemed the perfect approach. The "I Found It!" method for evangelism had the potential to painlessly, logically lead anyone—at least, anyone who was reasonably open to the gospel—from doubt to Jesus Christ. And it worked, apparently. Several people with whom my group spoke did make professions of faith. Of course, I have no idea whether those professions were genuine or not. But it felt great just to hear their continuing agreement as we worked our way closer and closer to the big question. I thought this was obviously a great way to evangelize.

In hindsight, the "I Found It!" campaign looks like nothing but an utter failure. Because the slogan had no meaning for those who didn't receive personal visits or who had no use for door-to-door evangelists, it was ridiculed out of hand by bumper stickers that answered, "Well, I Lost It!" and "You Can Keep It!" Worse, the campaign's whole approach was manipulative and insulting toward its intended audience; if Christianity is primarily about relationships, this approach to evangelism was *anti*-Christian. It was hit-and-run witnessing.

Still, that brush with a formalized witnessing "method" sparked some interest. Later, when my father returned from a visit to southern Florida with news of a fantastic new program for leading people to Christ, I was excited. I enrolled in our local church's training sessions as soon as they became available.

In the 1970s Evangelism Explosion, developed at Coral Ridge Presbyterian Church in Fort Lauderdale, Florida, was the new wave in winning people to Christ, and it grabbed the attention of church leaders across the country. But EE was not the fad that "I Found It!" was. There were important differences between the two. Evangelism Explosion relied heavily on Scripture memorization and face-to-face discussion. And while it required learning a step-by-step process for moving from one point to the next—say, from the fact that all have sinned and fallen short of the glory of God to the fact that by grace we can be saved through faith—it was flexible in its approach. Most importantly, it was honest. Intended as a tool for church workers who followed up on visitors and inquirers with in-home visits, EE never tried to look like anything but a serious, logical discussion of humanity's sinfulness and God's loving response through Jesus Christ.

But there's that word again: *logic*. Though I believe my father is still a supporter of Evangelism Explosion (and, fervently, of evangelism in general), I can't shake the memory of something he once told me: "I never knew anyone who became a Christian because of a logical discussion."

That is truly good news for the mentally handicapped, because logic is vain where they are concerned. If it were a prerequisite for faith, they would have little chance to gain it.

In fact, it's likely that all of us have days when we want less logic, less discourse, less complex thought. What we want instead is to laugh, to hear a story, to talk about *us*. Friendship, not factual data. Relationship, not reasoning. Evangelistic campaigns that grab us by the arm and hustle us unerringly from point A to point B to point C don't meet us where we live. We might buy insurance that way, but we certainly won't buy the gospel. And chances are, we'd rather buy insurance from someone who at least knows our face and maybe the names of our spouse and children, not a door-to-door hit-and-runner. That's why "I Found It!" foundered. And that's why Evangelism Explosion will work best in situations where church workers don't just present the memorized material but commit themselves to establishing relationships with the people they visit.

Not surprisingly, that is also the method that works best with the mentally handicapped. As we build relationships with them and establish friendships with them, we can come to know them as well-rounded human beings, not merely as souls to win or as "poor handicapped people" whom, as Christians, we are obliged to help. That is very much in the style of Jesus' own approach to outreach.

Jesus, unfortunately, had no committees to help Him decide how He should minister. He also was hindered by a lack of scientific formulas, research statistics, and catchy slogans. But He did have this: an extreme and sincere interest in people's lives and personalities. He was so interested in people and their needs that He did not wait for them to come to Him in the synagogue—He met them where they lived. He met the adulterous woman beside the well, where she was waiting. He met a tax collector named Zacchaeus in the tree where he was perched. He met fishermen along the shore, amidst their boats. Yes, He was interested in their souls, turning every conversation to spiritual matters, probing people's hearts. But His Father did not create only their souls. He also fashioned their minds and their personalities, setting the spark to their interests and passions. It did not take people long at all to recognize that Jesus embodied something far different from the norm. And far better.

It is not accidental that when some Christians seek to weigh the validity of another's faith commitment, they ask, "Do you have a personal relationship with Jesus Christ?" Worship habits, Bible reading, prayer, regular devotions— all have some importance. But relying on such things without an underlying personal relationship with Jesus is like building our dreamhouse in a field of quicksand. We've probably done some wonderful things with the structure, but we've overlooked the most vital element for long-term success. Eternal life begins with a relationship.

Likewise, this book began with a relationship—the relationship between me and my sister.

Barbara is my big sister, with everything that title implies. She looked out for me when I was small, and I followed her everywhere. I can't remember my first memory of my sister; my memories are mixed up with family stories, slow-motion 8mm movie images, black-and-white photographs, and my imagination.

I wish now that I could recall those days when Barbara was my leader, my caretaker, my friend. I regret the day when she slipped from being my big sister to being my mentally handicapped sister. That change doesn't seem quite right. She's older; she should be the wiser one. She should be able to continue leading, caring for, and befriending me. Instead, as I've grown older, those options have disappeared. Or perhaps I've just usurped them.

Barbara has gone through phases where she will do an activity—like toss a comb up in the air and catch it—continuously. I have had no problem telling her to stop doing that. When, during a particularly dark period in her life, she needed to stay in a nursing home catering to the mentally handicapped, I had little difficulty telling my parents that I thought she should be sent there. I have not always been a thoughtful leader and caretaker where Barbara is concerned. Friendship is something else again.

Part of my reason for writing this book was to learn more about mental retardation, its processes, its causes and effects, and the way it alters one's ability to understand and process information. In the process I hoped that by researching, writing, and talking with folks who were working with and ministering to the mentally handicapped, I might understand my own sister better and develop a different kind of love for her.

UNLOCKING LOVE

I have marveled at the work of those who feel called to serve the mentally handicapped. Many of them have relatives who are mentally disabled, and their work is touched with the compassion of a loving sibling. They crouch beside a sheltered-workshop employee and teach him to count the number of screws that should be packed in a box. They sit patiently beside a young woman at the nursing home and hold a spoonful of soup to her lips because she cannot move her arms. They supervise a group home for the mentally handicapped, adopt a mentally disabled child, or counsel a handicapped couple contemplating marriage. They lead a church choir that includes two mentally handicapped members, and they teach a Sunday school class especially designed for the mentally disabled. They have a love that sees beyond the handicap, sees beyond any personal disappointments, and removes the blinders that would allow them to ignore those in their care.

Such a love has not often been a part of my life, even where my own sister was concerned. It was my hope that this book would help me to change, to become a more giving Christian and a better brother. After all, Barbara may be fine now—and she is—but what about the future? My parents, like every parent who has a mentally handicapped child, wonder what might happen to her when they are no longer around to give her support. I wonder too. She will be my responsibility. She will be dependent on her younger brother. Will I love her like my parents do? Will I be concerned for her welfare as they are? Will she know that I do indeed love her?

Is it unfair for me to say that only time will tell? After all, living nearly 500 miles away makes any regular, personal contact impossible, and Barbara has never been much for talking on the telephone. And even though I make my living writing, I have never been good at keeping up with correspondence.

But I do believe there is hope for the future. I certainly have changed during the year I thought about and worked with this topic. I have even been encouraged to be more demonstrative verbally about my feelings toward my family. Still, it may be that the leadership for building a better relationship with my sister will actually begin with Barbara. The incident that makes me think so happened when my wife, Sylvia, and I last visited my parents in southern Illinois. Once we've loaded up the car to leave, it has been my father's habit to gather Mom, Sylvia, me, and Barbara (if she's visiting) in a circle for prayer. He then thanks God for our visit, prays that we will have a safe journey home, and asks God to bless us in all of our activities. Afterwards, Sylvia and I say our good-byes, hug Mom and Dad, and leave. This last time, however, Barbara met me at the door as we were walking out, said, "Bye, Bob," and gave me a hug. As Sylvia and I pulled out of the driveway, I turned to her and said, "Well, I think you've just witnessed a historic moment. As far as I know, that's the first time my sister and I have ever embraced." On the one hand, I felt slightly ashamed to admit that. On the other, it seemed as if a new door had opened between us. And Barbara was the one who unlocked it.

WHAT IF . . .

Actually I hoped to accomplish three things with this book. First, I hoped to make plain the fact that the mentally handicapped are human beings with real spiritual needs. Second, I hoped to present ways that the church at large can respond to those needs through a basic attitude of openness and acceptance, and through specific programs created to address the special needs of the mentally disabled. Last, I hoped to convey the rich spiritual growth that we, as ministers to the mentally handicapped, can experience because of our outreach.

Yet even if we do become more understanding, more flexible in our programming, and more deeply committed to God as a result of our work with the mentally disabled, that doesn't mean we will never catch ourselves stopping in midsentence during a Sunday school class and asking ourselves, "What if . . . ?"

"What if Sheila had been born normal? What might she have become?"

"What if William had been my own son? How would I have reacted?"

"What if God chose not to allow mental handicaps to happen? Would the world be better for it?"

For all the love we may have for the mentally handicapped, I think it would be extraordinary if we were never to ask ourselves—or God—these questions.

Is this pity for the mentally handicapped? I don't believe so. Pity will fade as we establish relationships. The "What if?" question does not deny the mentally disabled their successes or wonder with a sigh when they will be able to accomplish something worthwhile. But we don't ask "What if?" unemotionally either. We ask it with sorrow for a sinful world where disease and accident can alter the course of life even before birth. We may ask it with regret for a parent's wrong choices during pregnancy. We may even ask "What if?" when our work with the mentally handicapped has worn us down, when we are all out of special teaching techniques and patience.

Often the "What if?" question cannot simply be asked and answered. The emotions that gave rise to it will wash upon us again and again as we spend time with the mentally disabled. Prayer and finding additional support for the ministry can help. And there are other ways of dealing with "What if?" in our lives. Some are positive and healthy— such as Bible reading, evaluating our own expectations of the mentally handicapped, discussing the issue with a friend. Likewise, some answers to the question can stop our effectiveness cold, damaging our ability to look beyond "what might have been" to see the reality before us, to work practically with *what is*. Kathleen Lukens, writing in *Guideposts*, told of a friend's unusual answer to "What if?" and how it changed her outlook completely.

> A close friend surprised me by announcing her plans to go to Lourdes to bathe her young handicapped son in the curative waters. . . . She'd been saving up for the trip for a solid year.
>
> Marie and I had helped each other through our late 30s. Her Billy and my David were born brain-damaged. They were both the fourth of five children, and a unique source of joy and grief. Marie and I had been through many trials together.
>
> It would be a difficult trip for her, alone with an unpredictable boy. . . . But even if there was only a slim chance that the waters of Lourdes would miraculously help Billy and transform him into a normal child, she must have felt she owed it to him to try. . . .
>
> Almost before I had time to miss her, Marie returned. She came back with a spring in her step and a new vitality in running her teeming household. She was more patient. There was a peace about her.
>
> Billy, on the other hand, seemed exactly the same.
>
> I was puzzled. As the weeks went by, I kept expecting Marie to tell me what had happened at Lourdes. But I didn't dare ask. The trip had obviously been a private experience. She didn't have to come out and tell me of her inner struggle. I knew.
>
> I loved my David, but I wanted him to be like other kids. How often had I thought, *Wouldn't it be wonderful if David were a normal child? A completely different child?* Other parents might wish their sons were better students or more athletic, their daughters less moody or more ambitious. Those weren't monumental changes, like what I wanted for David. What I wanted for my son would take a miracle.

At last the situation arose in which Kathleen heard herself asking the question she had been putting off: "Do you think the Lourdes water worked for Billy?"

> "You don't understand," Marie said slowly. "I didn't dip him in the waters. When it came time to do it, I just couldn't." . . .
>
> The word came out in a whisper: "Why?" I asked her.
>
> "Because I love him the way he is. Even if he'll never be the way I dreamed he'd be," Marie said, "I still love my son."

Marie was touched enough by "What if?" to commit an act of faith. But when her faith effected change, the results surprised her closest friend.

> A healing *had* taken place at Lourdes. And now it touched me. My child was from God. If someday, by some miracle, David were different, or "normal," I would praise God for his healing. And I'd love David—but no more than I loved him at this very moment.

There may be days when we dread the extra effort required to reach the mentally handicapped, when we grow impatient with the speed of their progress and their limited skills.

The same feelings can happen in our own spiritual lives. We have valleys, questions, struggles. But the key to Christian growth is knowing that our emotions have little to do with the actual work of God in our lives. And so we go on, slogging our way through whatever darkness we are experiencing, hoping—sometimes blindly—that God is in control, watching over us, and that eventually we'll reach the light. That same sort of trust despite appearances can lead us through our down times in our outreach to the mentally handicapped. And God will continue to work through us, regardless of how we feel at the moment.

REFLECTIONS

It is less difficult, I think, to put the "What if?" question behind you when you are not a relative of a mentally handicapped person, when your interactions with the mentally disabled are friend to friend rather than mother to daughter or brother to brother. Family members may wrestle for a long time with their feelings, their regrets, and the difference between what might have been and what is.

I still wrestle with these feelings. I may have a better understanding of mental handicaps, a deeper respect for those Christians who are actively seeking to work with the mentally disabled, a deeper respect for the mentally handicapped themselves. But the fact remains that my sister, Barbara, is mentally handicapped. And that fact has altered the life of my whole family.

A week before this writing, on June 21, Barbara celebrated her forty-third birthday. I'm not good with remembering dates; I'm not sure I'd remember hers if I couldn't link it with being the longest day of the year. I'm not much better with ages. Whenever I tell anyone my parents' ages, I have to give them plus or minus a year; I'm never exactly sure. But I remember Barbara's age because we are ten years apart. She turned forty-three in the summer; I turn thirty-three in the fall. In ways big and small, she helps to define who I am. That has never changed.

Barbara passed on to me her love for the Beatles (and her collection of original 45s and albums). She introduced me to her friends, men and women whose personalities would stay with me vividly for life. She still makes me smile as she laughs at the story of how, as a very young boy, I told our grandfather, "Eat your crust, boy!" after he'd finished a piece of pie.

And I remember the not-so-good times. The sound of her running up the steps, slamming her bedroom door, and loudly crying. The day she came home from the workshop to discover that all of her belongings had been packed in the car, that she needed more professional care than my parents could give her and was headed for a nursing home. (It had been talked about before, but Barbara hadn't taken my parents seriously.)

Good times and bad, we are brother and sister. Barbara and Bobby. Neither of us would be the same today without the other. For that, I thank God. I would hope that Barbara would say the same.

A SPECIAL INVITATION

I would hope you, too, would be able to thank God as you minister to the mentally handicapped—whether that means sharing the gospel with a daughter, a nephew, a neighbor, or a friend at church. The church has come a long way from the early attitude that the mentally disabled are either demon-possessed or God's special messengers on earth. We have made immense progress since the days when the words "educable mentally handicapped" would have been deemed ludicrous. The church has made some big steps forward. Until the twentieth century, the church was at the forefront: leading seminars, founding (and funding) institutions, treating, training, and evangelizing.

That's no longer the case. Like so many other areas,

mental retardation has fallen away from the church and has become the domain of medicine, education, and social services. Not that these groups do not do some fine work. But unless an individual doctor, teacher, or social worker is a Christian, she or he may not find the time to discuss spiritual matters with a mentally handicapped individual. If we believe that the mentally disabled do have spiritual lives—and can experience a saving spiritual understanding—Christians owe it to the world to *make* the time for ministry—to entwine our lives with the mentally handicapped and thereby nurture one another.

Edna Moore Schultz, in her book *They Said Kathy Was Retarded*, wrote the following description of her own daughter:

> Kathleen was a lovely little Christian girl. Since babyhood she had gone with us to Sunday school and church. . . .
>
> Kathy listened intently when the pastor gave the message. . . . She heard him tell of the love of God, and she knew God loved her. He said that in order to go to Heaven, it was necessary to repent of one's sins and take Jesus into the heart. Sometimes at the close of the sermon, Pastor Swartz would ask, "Is there anyone here who would like to receive the Lord Jesus Christ?" Kathy's little hand would be raised. She wanted to receive the Lord.
>
> Pastors do not always notice the children who respond to this invitation, but that did not deter Kathy. She whispered to me, "I have to see Pastor." . . .
>
> She became obsessed with the notion that she must make him understand that she loved the Lord. She would go to him after every service, take his hand, and give him a little curtsy in her quaint way. "Pastor, I love the Lord," she would say.
>
> Pastor Swartz was pleasant to her and assured her,

"I know you do, Kathy." But, each time the invitation was given, she was sure he gave it for her.

Why reach out to the mentally handicapped? Because they can teach us to see God with fresh eyes, to hear His invitation anew, and to feel its claim upon our hearts with renewed commitment.

In the late 1970s Jerry Estes, of the Christian music group The Good News Circle, wrote a song entitled "If I'd Been the Only One" that spoke to me the moment I first heard it.

> If I'd been the only one
> Alone in my despair,
> Would You still have come for me?
> If I'd been the only one
> Thinking no one cared,
> Would You still have come for me?
> If I'd been the only one. . . .

A second verse of questioning is followed by a chorus in which the answer is vividly evident:

> Every tear He cried was just for me.
> When they pierced His side, He bled for me.
> And as He slowly died on calvary,
> I get the feeling He was thinking of me.

> If I'd been the only one
> Alone in my despair,
> Still You would have come for me.
> If I'd been the only one
> Thinking no one cared,
> Still You would have come for me.
> If I'd been the only one. . . .
> To You I am the only one.

I do not doubt the reality of that song. The story of the gospel is the story of God saving a race that doesn't deserve to be saved. Can it matter whether that race numbers into the hundreds of billions or whether it consists of a solitary member?

There may be only one mentally handicapped person in our community. But we can have an incredible impact on the life of that one person. By reaching out in the name of Christ, we can share the love that forgives, that changes lives, that accepts. My prayer is that all of us—regardless of our mental aptitudes or our status in the eyes of others—will find love, hope, and shelter under God's wings.

Sources

The following sources were especially helpful in the writing of this book.

BOOKS AND MAGAZINES

All God's Children, Revised Edition by Gene Newman and Joni Eareckson Tada. Grand Rapids, MI: Zondervan, 1993.

Alzheimer's: Caring for Your Loved One, Caring for Yourself by Sharon Fish. Batavia, IL: Lion, 1990.

"For the Love of Peter" by Ginny Thornburgh. *Guideposts*. October 1993, pp. 2-5.

A History of Mental Retardation by R. C. Scheerenberger. Baltimore: Paul H. Brookes, 1983.

A History of the Care and Study of the Mentally Retarded by Leo Kanner. Springfield, IL: Charles C. Thomas, 1964.

How to Teach Special Students by Joan Dubberke. St. Louis: Concordia, 1992.

The Journey Through AIDS by Debra Jarvis. Batavia, IL: Lion, 1992.

The Lambs of Libertyville by Tim Unsworth. Chicago: Contemporary Books, 1990.

Look at Me, Please Look at Me by Dorothy Clark, Jane Dahl, Lois Gonzenbach. Elgin, IL: David C. Cook, 1973.

Mental Defectives: Their History, Treatment and Training by Martin W. Barr, M.D. Philadelphia: P. Blakiston's Son & Co., 1904.

"A Perfect Child" by Kathleen Lukens. *Guideposts*. February 1994, pp. 14-15.

Retarded Children: God's Children by Sigurd D. Peterson. Philadelphia: The Westminster Press, 1960.

77 Dynamic Ideas for the Christian Education of the Handicapped by James O. Pierson. Cincinnati: Standard, 1977.

Teach Me, Please Teach Me, Revised Edition by Dorothy Clark, Jane Dahl, Lois Gonzenbach. Elgin, IL: David C. Cook, 1981.
They Said Kathy Was Retarded by Edna Moore Schultz. Chicago: Moody Press, 1963.
When a Child Is Different by Dr. Maria Egg. New York: The John Day Company, 1964.

CURRICULUM

Breakthrough
Bethesda Lutheran Home & Services
700 Hoffmann Drive
Watertown, WI 53094
(414) 261-3050

Concordia Publishing House
3558 South Jefferson Avenue
St. Louis, MO 63118
(314) 268-1000

Friendship Ministries
2850 Kalamazoo Avenue SE
Grand Rapids, MI 49560
(616) 246-0842

Annotated Bibliography

The bulk of the following bibliography is adapted from a research project entitled *Serving Mentally Impaired People: A Resource Guide for Pastors and Church Workers*, compiled by Gerald Oosterveen and Bruce L. Cook and published by David C. Cook in 1983. It is reprinted courtesy of Charlene Heibert and the David C. Cook Foundation. (Although I have adapted the material for this book, the evaluations reflect the opinions of the project's researchers. Entries noted with an asterisk are original to this work.)

Popular, or "trade," books about the spiritual needs of the mentally handicapped do not have long in-print lives. From a practical standpoint, the need is simply too small. The majority of books that follow are evidence of that fact: nearly every one is now out of print (as is the research project from which I've taken their descriptions).

So why mention them at all?

First, even books that are "out of print" are still available in public and church libraries, used bookstores, and private collections. One publisher I spoke with even told me they would be willing to reprint the title I asked about if I would purchase at least ten copies. I couldn't use ten copies, but a church might. If a book catches your attention, seek it out.

Second, even so-called old books can offer important personal insights and instruction. The *medical* understanding of mental handicaps has changed substantially over the years, but many aspects of the church's attitude toward the mentally disabled have not. Books from forty years ago may be just as relevant and informative as those published this year.

By turning to older titles you can discover topics or approaches that are not currently fashionable in publishing. For instance, the sixties and seventies saw a large number of first-person stories published by families with mentally handicapped children, describing how they coped and survived. Unless there's a unique "hook" to the story—a parent who is a celebrity, say—such books aren't generally being published today.

Also, the *history* of mental handicaps has not changed, and a number of books in this list provide interesting and useful historical background about the changing information and attitudes through the ages. I believe that knowledge leads to empathy and understanding; if this book—and particularly Chapter 2—has whetted your appetite to know more about the history of the mentally disabled, a number of books here would be good places to start.

Allen, David F., and Allen, Victoria S. *Ethical Issues in Mental Retardation: Tragic Choices/Living Hope.* Nashville: Abingdon Press, 1979, 172 pages.

Summary Sentence: "To create an informed public awareness of the ethical choices concerning persons with mental retardation in our technological society."

After an introductory chapter that defines mental handicaps and offers a historical overview, the book deals with specific ethical issues. Who should be born? Who should live? Where should they live? How should they live sexually? Problems of behavior modification are also discussed: How much control? Who should decide? Final chapters challenge the church to create a caring community and point toward a better future for mentally handicapped people.

Written from a Christian perspective, there is no denominational bias. It refers to biblical teachings and texts, and it adopts the technique of raising many issues without claiming dogmatic answers. It expresses the viewpoint that mentally handicapped persons have a right to life and a worthwhile place in society.

This book offers thoughtful advice on values and practices in bringing mentally handicapped people into the community. Technical terms are avoided, except for those in everyday usage, and the book capably contrasts differing views; after reading the material, readers must draw their own conclusions.

There is an excellent, eight-page bibliography. Materials for religious education are listed for Jewish, Protestant, and Catholic congregations. However, it should be noted that the resource list is now dated.

Association for Retarded Citizens. *Creating Positive Attitudes Among Non-Handicapped Students Toward Their Handicapped Peers.* Arlington, TX: 1980, 39 pages.

Summary Sentence: Reflects problems and issues discussed at a conference of professionals in the field of special education. While this book sets mainstreaming as an objective in serving mentally handicapped persons, it lists various obstacles to total integration. Most of the pamphlet suggests creative ways to improve attitudes and foster the acceptance of mentally disabled people. While public schools were the center of attention for this conference, the attitude problem was seen as a community-wide issue. As a result, Christian educators and parents will find useful ideas here.

Baumgartner, Diane Braunstein. *Melissa: The Story of a Very Special Baby.* Elgin, IL: David C. Cook, 1980, 113 pages.

Summary Sentence: This book describes the author's experiences as the foster mother of a mentally handicapped child. It traces Melissa's birth from the mother's point of view, placement from the social worker's point of view, and finally the child's brief life as seen through the sensitive eyes of the foster mother.

This book illustrates that while parents of disabled children can't expect a miracle to remove their child's handicap, they can rejoice in smaller miracles every day. It will help parents of mentally disabled children to realize that their misgivings over parenting a mentally handicapped child are not only natural, but also a spiritual challenge.

The text is very readable. Readers can't help but identify with the parents and foster parents in this story. In fact, they will be captured by the book and will share some difficult emotions. Of the valuable information this book offers to parents of mentally handicapped children, perhaps the most valuable suggestion is to depend on their faith. The author underlines the importance and strength of her own faith as she explains how she trusted God in allowing the baby she'd cared for to have a relationship with its real mother. Her risk in doing this resulted in unexpected spiritual rewards.

Black, Mary Maurice. *Teach Them As Jesus Did.* Watertown, NY: Watertown Catechetical Office, 1979, 95 pages.

Summary Sentence: A resource for persons working in religious special education.

This book includes background information about the nature and learning characteristics of mentally handicapped people as well as useful suggestions about religious education approaches, methods, and tools. Valuable resources, including books and pamphlets for background reading, teaching aids, films, pictures, and other materials, are included.

Prepared for religious special instruction within the Roman Catholic Church, this book actually could be used by anyone involved in the religious education of mentally handicapped people.

It is simply written and gives the most comprehensive treatment to the resources currently available. The section on methods contains brief suggestions, most of which are very practical. The reading list is inclusive. Since much Protestant literature is included, the handbook will also serve Protestants. In addition, much of the text has annotated bibliographical listings.

Board of Global Ministries. *The Church and Persons with Handicapping Conditions*. The United Methodist Church, 15 pages, 1979; no address or author is cited.

Summary Sentence: A brief but persuasive presentation of the need to "include, assimilate, receive the gifts, and respond to the needs of those with mental, physical, and/or psychologically handicapping conditions."

This booklet is directed toward United Methodists but also has value for other Christians. It is written by a number of persons who have personally faced handicapping conditions.

Bogardus, LaDonnas, ed. *Camping with Retarded Persons*. Nashville: Board of Education of the United Methodist Church, 1970, 46 pages.

Summary Sentence: Gives leaders practical tips on conducting church camps for mentally handicapped people. Every aspect of camping is covered: contacting parents, finding campers and counselors, where to go, what to do, what to eat, how to evaluate the program, and how to improve it.

The book assumes that the counselors, if not the campers, will be Christian. The camp situation offers opportunities for learning that are not possible in the regular experience of the mentally disabled. This book will be most useful to church leaders involved in camping and scouting; it assumes counselors know how to cook, start a fire, and draw on the book's collection of suggested games and activities. Helpful suggestions are given, but a novice may be frustrated by too-brief explanations. An appendix lists additional resources.

Buck, Pearl S., and Zarfoss, Gweneth. *The Gifts They Bring*. New York: The John Day Company, 1965, 156 pages.

Summary Sentence: Demonstrates that mentally handicapped people are not a burden on society. Instead, they make a positive contribution and bring spiritual gifts to those who pay attention.

The book begins with a brief survey of the history of mental retardation: early discoveries about mental ability, intelligence tests, research using mentally disabled persons as guinea pigs, and studies seeking the prevention of mental handicaps. It goes on to explain services that mentally disabled people need, including teaching programs, job training, living arrangements, and social responsibilities. Includes an extensive index.

The authors regard mentally handicapped people as individuals who should be allowed to interact with society to the fullest extent possible while maintaining their unique identities. The term *mainstreaming* was not yet coined when the book was written, but the authors would endorse it, at least in principle. This book would prove helpful for Christian educators because the book depicts mentally disabled people not only as recipients but also as contributors. It is simply written and easy to read.

While much information is dated, the book is worth reading for its unique view that mentally handicapped people have gifts to contribute to society. A superior literary style makes the volume worth the relatively little amount of time it takes to read.

Carlson, Bernice Wells, and Ginglend, David. *Play Activities for the Retarded Child*. Nashville: Abingdon Press, 1981, 224 pages.

Summary Sentence: Presents activities for untrained leaders to use in helping the mentally handicapped child grow and learn. This book explains the need for play as an aid to development, then offers detailed descriptions of types of play: informal, imaginative, imitative, table work, handicrafts, music, and games.

The authors believe that mentally disabled children deserve the opportunity to develop their potential through guidance and discipline. The result will contribute to mentally handicapped persons' self-esteem and will help them have fun even as they find a place in their communities. The book is written primarily for parents working with a mentally disabled child, especially one whose mental age is below age six. Recreation leaders and teachers also will benefit from this book.

This is an excellent resource of activities to develop a child's social and physical skills. It has value as one portion of a Christian education setting, recognizing that the Christian teaching would have to be done separately from playtime.

Clark, Dorothy; Dahl, Jane; and Gonzenbach, Lois. *Look at Me, Please Look at Me*. Elgin, IL: David C. Cook, 1973, 125 pages.

Summary Sentence: This book fosters understanding of and love for mentally handicapped children who, despite their often unattractive appearances, are persons created by God.

Under three major divisions—Faith, Hope, and Love—the authors describe twenty-nine true incidents involving mentally handicapped people in worship services, Christmas pageants, and field trips. A specific concept of the Christian faith is highlighted. Through these incidents the book emphasizes that God's love is very real to handicapped people and to those who help them know God. However, the authors omit a description of mental retardation itself. Incidents are described with the conviction that God acts in the ordinary events of daily life. No reference is made to any specific denomination; the perspective is Protestant and evangelical. The authors intend to help people relate to and work with the handicapped. However, lack of specificity limits the book's usefulness as a resource for starting a class for mentally disabled people.

The book is readable and avoids technical terms. The primary contribution is the book's biographical account of how the authors overcame their reluctance to work with handicapped people, discovering in the process that handicapped people are indeed unique and can contribute to their community.

Clark, Dorothy; Dahl, Jane; and Gonzenbach, Lois. *Teach Me, Please Teach Me*. Elgin, IL: David C. Cook, 1974, 142 pages.

Summary Sentence: Brings the reality of Jesus Christ into the daily fabric of each mentally handicapped student's life.

This companion volume to *Look at Me, Please Look at Me* presents the curriculum ideas used in classes taught by the authors. An introduction briefly describes how to teach mentally handicapped people, use a curriculum, and set up a program. The remainder of the book offers twelve lessons, each suggesting a pre-session activity, materials, lesson development, enrichment, and summary review questions. Lessons begin by using familiar, ordinary objects and then weave in a biblical concept. Helpful illustrations accompany each lesson to guide the teacher in preparation.

Lessons are designed for groups having ten or more students, but the book will also apply to smaller groups. Authors assume that a special class for mentally handicapped people works best. While they encourage contact with other students in the church school, they do not mix them indiscriminately. No technical terms are employed, so this book is useful for teachers who lack formal training. Lessons proceed from the known to the unknown and are clearly outlined. One weakness is that no distinction is made between types of mental handicaps; consequently, the leader does not know whether the lessons are for use with trainable or educable students. Teachers will also have to determine whether the book is suitable for older or younger students.

Clarke, Bill. *Enough Room for Joy.* **New York: The Paulist Press, 1974, 143 pages.**

Summary Sentence: Describes the author's stay at Jean Vanier's L'Arche (The Ark), a French community where mentally handicapped and normal persons live and work together. There the author discovers that an atmosphere of love and acceptance can richly bless both the mentally handicapped and the normal through involvement.

The book describes the philosophy on which the community is based, the process by which it came into being (since then, several similar communities have sprung up), and the struggles and joys experienced by those living at The Ark. Particularly emphasized is the inseparable relationship between worship and work. Written for the general public, this book will have special appeal for the religious community.

Despite its Roman Catholic orientation, Protestants will profit from this book. The author, a Jesuit, makes frequent references to Catholic dogma and liturgy. Both founder Jean Vanier and author Bill Clarke seem drawn toward a mystical, contemplative, monastic lifestyle. While Protestants may be unfamiliar with some liturgy and practices, the book is well-written and easily understood.

However, pastors, parents, and church-school teachers will find nothing here that has direct benefit for the training and teaching of the mentally handicapped. The book is significant because it is one of very few to underscore the importance of religion in the life of handicapped people. Vanier has gone beyond the current trend toward incorporating mentally disabled people in the community by suggesting that normal and handicapped people live together, relating to each other as worthy persons. The L'Arche communities succeed because human needs are reduced to basics: the need for love and the need to do something useful and find meaning in life. The resulting book is a valuable contribution to the current discussion of where and how mentally handicapped people can live among us, even though not all persons have the temperament to live in an "Ark."

Duckert, Mary. *Open Education Goes to Church.* **Philadelphia: The Westminster Press, 1976, 140 pages.**

Summary Sentence: To provide encouragement, guidelines, and specific information for those seeking to make their church school more effective. This book explains the "open classroom" concept and offers suggestions on how to develop a learning center for various grades. Models are offered for small churches, which include several age groups in one classroom setting. One chapter deals with the challenge of including handicapped children in the classrooms. The final chapter offers suggestions for improving successful programs.

This book advocates the open-classroom concept, which is fairly common in public schools. The section on church school for handicapped children advocates the mainstreaming concept, with some qualifications. Each suggested innovation attempts to stress biblical instruction. The open-classroom concept is explained clearly, without professional jargon.

Designed primarily for teachers, the book could also prove a handy resource for pastors, church board members, and parents. It will be especially useful in settings where the mentally disabled are included with normal Sunday school members.

There is much in this book that should stimulate those struggling with uninspiring classroom situations to try learning centers, activity centers, and intergenerational learning events—letting readers know that such programs have been found workable and attractive in churches across the country. It is not the book, however, to help those planning to set up separate classes for severely mentally handicapped people.

Hahn, Hans R., and Raasch, Werner H. *Helping the Retarded to Know God*. St. Louis: Concordia, 1969, 112 pages.

Summary Sentence: To help train church members to teach special education classes. Nearly half the text is devoted to describing mentally handicapped people and how they learn. The remaining chapters set the context for Christian education in the church and offer guidelines for evaluating and selecting curriculum materials.

The authors assert that all of God's children, including mentally disabled people, are meant to grow in Christian life and faith, and their presentation is very readable. Although this introduction tries to cover much ground in a short space, the information is presented clearly.

Church workers will appreciate this thorough, although dated, introduction to serving mentally handicapped people in the church.

Hawley, Gloria H. *How to Teach the Mentally Retarded*. Wheaton, IL: Scripture Press, 1978, 48 pages.

Summary Sentence: To give practical help in presenting God's Word to mentally handicapped persons; to help remove some of the myths and the stigma attached to working with the mentally disabled; to communicate the dignity, worth, and spiritual potential of mentally handicapped persons; and to stir readers to open their hearts and church doors to these special people.

The needs of mentally handicapped children are discussed, as are parents', home, teachers', class, and church involvement. The author writes from the perspective of one who believes that God's Word is the unchanging plumb line for mankind. The resulting book offers valuable insights into mental handicaps and its challenges.

Teachers will enjoy the material, especially the strong biblical emphasis. (The author advocates the use of Scripture wherever possible, even in music.) An excellent section on how to set up a class is geared to a large church able to develop a program involving twenty to thirty mentally disabled persons.

All in all, this is a very clearly written book and a strong, positive witness. However, there is one flaw: a brief passage speaks of a mentally handicapped girl who accepted Christ and then no longer needed either her special Sunday school or her public school. This is unbelievable, and suggesting that it is a reasonable goal is bound to raise unrealistic hopes in parents and teachers.

Krentel, David P. ". . . *Unto the Least of These* . . .": A *Survey of Ministry to the Retarded.* D.Min. paper, Dallas Theological Seminary, 1980, 111 pages.

Summary Sentence: To explain ministries, materials, and the meaning of Christian service to mentally handicapped people. It includes an introduction, rationale for ministry, survey of literature, transcript of a discussion with mentally handicapped people on why God made them as He did, an annotated bibliography, declarations, and addresses for various agencies that provide (or could be expected to provide) services for mentally disabled individuals.

The author thoroughly develops a biblical mandate for church service to mentally handicapped people, stressing the idea that churches must offer such services as a consequence of counseling parents not to abort a fetus diagnosed as abnormal. The theological comments will be of interest to pastors, and the comprehensive survey of services and ministries will help acquaint new church workers with services and resources available in this field. Also, the transcript of the discussion with mentally disabled people, exploring why God made them as He did, offers unique insight into how the mentally handicapped view God in relationship to themselves.

Lind, Miriam S. *No Crying He Makes*. Scottdale, PA: Herald Press, 1972, 93 pages.

Summary Sentence: A unique perspective—the point of view of a person who chose to be the foster mother of a brain-injured child. This book relates the author's impressions as her child grows, providing a testimony to the mother's personal and spiritual strength in her conviction that love conquers all.

Parents of mentally handicapped children will identify with this story.

Martin, C. Lewis, and Travis, John T. *Exceptional Children: A Special Ministry*. Valley Forge, PA: Judson Press, 1968, 63 pages.

Summary Sentence: Stresses that the educational ministry of the church should include all exceptional children, whether they are mentally, physically, or emotionally different.

The authors describe many types of exceptional children, stress the need for special programs, and suggest guidelines for starting dedicated ministries. A "last word" urges churches to include as many children as possible. Appendixes include an enrollment form and a survey form.

Although produced by the publishing arm of the American Baptist Churches, there is no particular denominational bias. The need for special classes is based upon social and biblical principles. The text stresses mainstreaming mentally handicapped children with normal children.

Written for clergy and laity involved in the church's

educational ministry, the book is readable, apart from the presence of a few technical terms in the section describing the various disabilities. However, the book's strength lies in its description of various disabilities, including mental handicaps as well other handicapping conditions. The book's thesis is that there should be room for all children in the church school. Its weakness is its brevity; the length makes it impossible to go beyond very generalized guidelines for a program for exceptional children.

Muller-Fahrenholz, Geiko, ed. *Partners in Life: The Handicapped and the Church*. Geneva: The World Council of Churches, 1979, 184 pages.
Summary Sentence: In the words of editor Geiko Muller-Fahrenholz: "This book is . . . a beginning in an attempt to discover anew the wholeness of the family of God in and with the handicapped" and to help normal and mentally handicapped people to sustain each other, as partners in life, to the glory of God.

This collection of articles and personal testimonies includes theological rationale and practical guidance for those who work with handicapped people. It also summarizes examples of integration between handicapped and normal people. The authors stress the worldwide problem of disability as a demand and a challenge to the church—its theology and worship—and part of the responsibility of the church—to treat the handicapped as partners rather than objects of charity. "Whoever treats them as [objects] robs them of their worth and disregards the fact that they, too, are created in the image of God." This book will help sensitize Christians and church leaders to the needs of handicapped people.

While much of the language is quite simple, some sections require thoughtful theological reflection. Overall this is a challenging blend of faith and practice. Each article must be read individually, however; authors do not always see eye to eye. Leslie Newbegin, for example, says that Jesus treated illness and disability as the work of the devil, while Ulrich Bach, with equal appeal to Scripture, claims that "as creator, God is also the author of events which we can only describe as disastrous." While the book omits specific programs, it does confront the church with questions of who we are, who the handicapped are, and how all of us are contributors and partners in the church. This thoughtful book can be profitably used by members of all denominations.

*Newman, Gene, and Tada, Joni Eareckson. *All God's Children: Ministry with Disabled Persons*, Revised Edition. Grand Rapids, MI: Zondervan, 1993, 126 pages.

Summary Sentence: ". . . that churches across the country will become better equipped to minister to persons with disabilities. This manual is filled with motivational, inspirational, and instructional helps designed to assist you and your church in preparing and conducting disability ministry."

Writing from the perspective that God does not create accidents, the authors provide practical guidelines for outreach to people with disabilities, including mental handicaps, deafness, physical disabilities, visual impairments, and learning disabilities. Interestingly, the text includes two chapters that discuss the importance of the pastor's support of the ministry and the valuable roles played by volunteers. It closes with a ten-step plan for getting started, an interview form for disabled students that would alert teachers to important information ("Do you have seizures?" "What is your medication schedule?"), and a brief chart that links special-needs groups with the types of ministry needs they may be experiencing.

Although mental handicaps is not the main focus of this book—appearing specifically in only one chapter—the authors provide basic, practical information that will prove helpful to those considering a ministry to the mentally disabled. The more general-interest first third of the book also offers valuable background information that applies as much to the mentally handicapped as to any other special-needs group.

Noland, Robert L., ed. *Counseling Parents of the Mentally Retarded*. Springfield, IL: Charles C. Thomas, 1970, 404 pages.

Summary Sentence: To emphasize parents' and siblings' need for emotional support and guidance as they learn to accept their handicapped child. Thirty-one articles cover parental attitudes and feelings, explaining how to inform parents that their child will be mentally handicapped and how to help them through group counseling.

The book also covers social casework, institutionalization, pastoral counseling, and genetic counseling. Particular attention is given to the problem of guilt. (Note, however, that because of its age it will not take into consideration the ramifications of contemporary parents' legal, but not ethical, right to choose an abortion for a fetus that is diagnosed early on with handicapping conditions.) Appendixes provide information about parent associations, clinical programs for children, and audiovisual materials on mental handicaps.

The editor is convinced that proper information, linked with sympathetic follow-up support, will alleviate much of the initial trauma parents experience when they learn their child is mentally disabled. Intended for "professional and paraprofessional workers who are asked to aid the parents of a mentally handicapped child," the most technical language appears in the section on genetic counseling. Other chapters are quite readable, though style and language naturally vary among authors.

This book is invaluable in emphasizing feelings rather than clinical aspects of mental handicaps. Sections on parental feelings and pastoral counseling provide insights into the emotional and religious struggles that parents experience, showing unusual understanding in its continual reaffirmation that helpers must be cautious and gentle, accepting not merely the parents but also the child. Noland has collected valuable information that would normally be unavailable to the average reader.

Petersen, Sigurd D. *Retarded Children: God's Children*. Philadelphia: The Westminster Press, 1960, 152 pages.

Summary Sentence: To create positive feelings toward mentally handicapped persons in the community by writing about mentally disabled children who live in an institution. The author describes some adjustment pains and learning disabilities that mentally handicapped people have suffered, particularly in the years of neglect prior to the book's publication.

Petersen stresses that mentally handicapped people need care, training, love, and religious activities, especially learning that God cares for them and that Jesus wants to be their Savior. He explains some feelings and fears commonly experienced by parents of mentally disabled children. A theology of mental handicaps is presented along with a challenge for new potential in the church's ministry to mentally disabled children. (However, not all Christians would agree with Petersen's discussion of the new birth on pages 110-111.)

The author reasons that religious values can be passed along to mentally disabled people through teaching and relationships, and that the church must relate to these persons and claim them for Christ. He adopts a Lutheran approach to the covenant of grace and the sacraments. The book offers insights into the nature of mentally handicapped people and offers suggestions on how they can learn, providing encouragement for those who wish to build a relationship between mentally disabled persons and their Savior.

The text is aimed at church leaders, church school teachers, the general public, and parents. It offers few teaching hints that are directly applicable to the church school, but the book is definitely worth reading for its general information. In fact, this is one of the first books ever written on the religious needs and potentials of mentally handicapped people. Readers must remember, however, that institutions are no longer the same as described in this publication. The community at large has also changed, with a new emphasis on accepting handicapped people.

Radtke, Frederick A. *Candles in the Night: Thirty-one Meditations for Persons Called by God to Bring Up a Handicapped Child.* St. Louis: Concordia, 1978, 83 pages.

Summary Sentence: To move parents of newborn handicapped infants from initial shock to the protection of God's grace. Includes thirty-one meditations, with Bible quotations from the *Good News Bible*, and a postscript by the author.

As the title implies, the author consoles new parents of a handicapped child by showing that the child is a unique challenge and a special calling from God. Holding to sacramentalist views, the author offers much-needed daily sustenance to parents who are shocked to learn they must bring up a handicapped child. The text is very readable. Himself the father of a mentally disabled child, and the editor of curricula for Christian education of mentally handicapped people, Dr. Radtke offers sensitively written meditations. Only a person who has shared the experience of parenting a handicapped child could write such relevant devotions.

Reed, Susan, ed. *Ministry to the Mentally Retarded.* Raleigh, NC: Department of Special Ministries (Mimeo), Baptist State Convention, no date, 70 pages.

Summary Sentence: Provides a rationale for ministry to the mentally handicapped, saying, "We have a mission because the gospel has a message to all."

The book describes mentally disabled persons, considering their characteristics and needs and their families. Step-by-step suggestions are presented for establishing a special education committee and finding teachers, space, equipment, and other resources. A section on learning stresses the roles of music, art, drama, and movement in the learning process. Sample curriculum units are provided on various topics. A list of Baptist churches in North Carolina already providing classes concludes the manual. While the material can be found in other books, this pamphlet conveniently puts it between two covers, saving valuable time.

*Schultz, Edna Moore. *They Said Kathy Was Retarded.* Chicago: Moody Press, 1963, 128 pages.

Summary Sentence: A mother's story of how her family was blessed through the birth of a daughter with Mongolism: "God sent a joy into our home, a little girl named Kathy."

This is the very personal story of how one family dealt with the shock of a mentally handicapped child and how that child eventually changed their lives for the better and deepened their faith in God. Against their doctor's advice, the Schultzes chose to bring their daughter home rather than institutionalize her. The story of their struggle for patience and their growing love for Kathy clearly mirrors Kathy's own physical struggles (with illnesses and a very weak heart), emotional struggles, and sincere faith. Once she is diagnosed with leukemia, and it is clear that she will not live long, Kathy herself tells her parents that she is ready to go to heaven. The book concludes with a selection of poems that were inspired by Kathy's life.

Towns, Elmer L., and Groff, Roberta L. *Successful Ministry to the Retarded.* Chicago: Moody Press, 1972, 144 pages.

Summary Sentence: To advocate that "the church's ministry is twofold: first, a ministry to the retardate himself; and second, a ministry to the family."

Part One describes mental handicaps by considering who trainable mentally handicapped persons are, how they learn, and whether they can be saved. Part Two gives excellent suggestions on choosing a program, teachers, and teaching methods. The text explains counseling for the mentally disabled person and his family, including siblings, while two appendixes cover the history and a definition of mental handicaps. The authors feel that trainable mentally disabled children can conceptualize basic religious truths and therefore should receive religious training.

While this book is for teachers and pastors, parents and others can also benefit from reading it. The main text is nontechnical, while the appendixes do introduce some technical terms. Professional and practical advice is conveyed in a down-to-earth manner. It is not immediately clear from the text what constitutes "success"—e.g., whether success is a well-attended program or one that brings pupils to publicly accept Christ. The book itself succeeds in covering some tensions inherent in programs for the mentally handicapped and in suggesting ways to resolve tensions and bring about acceptance and support for mentally disabled people within the church school program.

Welborn, Terry, and Williams, Stanley. *Leading the Mentally Retarded in Worship.* **St. Louis: Concordia, 1973, 31 pages.**

Summary Sentence: To help leaders provide meaningful worship opportunities for mentally handicapped persons. The authors set forth a rationale for special services and explain worship goals, planning, and activities. The text covers sacraments and counseling, and it presents actual messages used by the authors in services for the mentally disabled. It offers a concise summary of information on methods, pitfalls, and blessings, promoting congregational understanding and acceptance of the specific needs of mentally handicapped people.

This book should be part of every library on Christian education and worship for the handicapped.

Wilke, Harold H. *Creating the Caring Community.* **Nashville: Abingdon Press, 1980, 110 pages.**

Summary Sentence: To present congregational guidelines that attempt to meet the needs of handicapped individuals.

The text describes the fear and awkwardness people commonly feel when meeting physically or mentally disabled persons. It goes on to take a look at some principles and practices governing relationships between normal and handicapped persons in Bible times. Two chapters, "The Church Says Yes" and "The Church Says No," deal with ambivalence in the Christian community. The author moves beyond the ambivalence by identifying three marks of a caring congregation—faith, fellowship, and service. He elaborates by offering guidelines on starting and continuing church service to mentally handicapped people. And he demonstrates that even though Scripture affirms the value of each individual in the sight of God, leadership in accepting disabled persons in the community has passed from the church to secular society; he pleads for a reverse in the situation. The overall goals are well-defined, and suggested programs are broken down into manageable steps that will help churches provide total integration of all members.

Directed toward concerned members of the church, the book avoids technical language and is very readable. It makes for a worthwhile contribution to the growing list of materials dealing with handicapped persons and the church. The book is particularly relevant because Wilke based it on years of testing in pilot programs and his own experience with a physical disability.